# the raging skillet

## the true life story of chef rossi

### BY ROSSI

**THE FEMINIST PRESS**
AT THE CITY UNIVERSITY
OF NEW YORK
NEW YORK CITY

Published in 2015 by the Feminist Press
at the City University of New York
The Graduate Center
365 Fifth Avenue, Suite 5406
New York, NY 10016

feministpress.org

 This book was made possible thanks to a grant from New York
State Council on the Arts with the support of Governor Andrew
NYSCA Cuomo and the New York State Legislature.

First printing November 2015

Cover design by Jenifer Walter
Text design by Drew Stevens
Author photo by Eitan Shapira

Library of Congress Cataloging-in-Publication Data
Rossi, Chef.
  The Raging Skillet : the true life story of Chef Rossi / by Rossi.
    pages cm
ISBN 978-1-55861-902-9 (pbk.) — ISBN 978-1-55861-903-6 (ebook)
1.  Rossi, Chef. 2.  Cooks—United States—Biography. 3.  Jewish cooking.
4.  Raging Skillet (Catering service) I. Title.
  TX649.R674A3 2015
  641.5092—dc23
  [B]

2015012151

*It is to my mother,
Harriet Ruby Ross by way of Goldstein,
that I dedicate my book, my whisk,
my chutzpah, and my journey.*

# Contents

# Recipes

# the
# raging
# skillet

# How I Became a Foodie Superhero

There they are: my sheep, two hundred of them, at the Horowitz-Chang wedding. They kick back their chairs and smile, too full to do anything but sigh. It had been a grand affair in the turn-of-the-century, factory-cum-Soho–style loft in newly chic Long Island City. Countless celebrities had flocked to the venue: Donald Trump filmed *The Apprentice* there. *The Sopranos* used it to shoot scenes for its final season. And once, while combing through the warehouse's lower floors for the perfect antique tray, I bumped into David Cassidy.

As the owner and executive chef of The Raging Skillet, a cutting-edge catering company based in New York City, I rarely get calls to cater mainstream event spaces. But a nightclub in Gowanus, a factory in Queens, an old synagogue turned goth party space on the Lower East Side? That's where we hold court.

When I was a kid, I was the queen of nothing. My Orthodox parents kept a tight rein, preferring that I never left home except to marry a nice Jewish doctor, lawyer, or maybe a pharmacist.

These days, I marry lots of nice Jewish guys, sometimes to each other. And the occasional man does win my hand.

"Will you marry me?" a groom once asked, peering into the kitchen just as I sent out dessert.

"Hmmm. Didn't you just do that, oh, about five hours ago?" I deadpanned, while arranging a tray of rugelach.

"Yes! But that salmon! You have stolen my heart!"

Moments later, the mother of the bride emerged, holding a shopping bag filled with plastic containers. "If you don't mind," she says in her thick Brooklyn accent, decades of cigarette smoke rasping her vocals, "everything was so good, I figured it would be even better tomorrow!"

As I spooned in enough leftovers to feed a football team, I looked down at her microwaveable bowls and started to laugh.

Ah, the microwave, the contraption that started it all.

I can't say we had a happy family, but we ambled along through mild discontent, with occasional bursts of joy and nausea. Dad was a teacher. Mom was a former teacher and mathematician. My brother, Matt, was laying the foundation for his excruciatingly ordered life as an accountant and yes, a teacher. Sister Lily was perfecting her private language based on sounds chickens make. And I, not yet Rossi, was all potential, no pizzazz.

In 1977 the Big M arrived.

It seemed innocent at first, this televisionish appliance that warmed soup in seconds, but within days of owning that first microwave, my mom was obsessed. Gone was the beef goulash that simmered longer than most of my relationships; the overcooked roast chicken seasoned with black pepper, paprika, and guilt; the cabbage and noodle casseroles with enough butter for six heart attacks.

The shelves in the garage, once stocked with enough canned goods to feed Pittsburgh, now held only tiny square containers of microwaveable soup and popcorn. The freezer became a smorgasbord of items, previously recognizable only to astronauts, waiting to be passed through the Big M and turned into the feasts promised on their seductive labels. Seductive, yes, because surely that's what happened to my mom. She was seduced by an electrical lover, and the payback was far more rewarding than a measly marriage with children.

The payback was time.

I was there for her first epiphany, the moment she suspiciously added water to a dry mix, plopped it in the microwave, pressed "2-0-0," and out came a bowl of tomato soup.

"It's like magic!" she squealed. "Eat it! Eat it! Tell me if it's good!"

"It's, umm, okay," I said, scrounging for a handful of saltines to soak up the bland mush.

"It only took two minutes!" she shrieked in delight. "Twoooooooominutessssss!"

She was reborn. No more slaving over vats of chicken soup. No more long hours traveling to the farthest kosher butcher for the cheapest veal. This thing, this tiny box, was her salvation. But it also was the end of food as we knew it.

There had always been an intangible price tag on my mother's cooking. We were supposed to do something more than say thank you; we were supposed to gorge ourselves as though this were our last meal on earth. Getting fat was the least we could do. I handled this task nicely, except I preferred to think of myself as big boned.

"Look at my wrists! I'm big boned!" I'd announced to the bully at school who called me "fatty."

Mom was big boned, too. At five feet tall, weighing in at 295 pounds, she had bones that could fill out a muu-muu like nobody's business.

When the Big M arrived, we figured that if Mom didn't have to spend so much time simmering stews into oblivion, we wouldn't have to be quite so grateful. We might even be able to get away without having thirds . . .

What we should have done was smash the microwave with the nearest sledgehammer or cooled-off meatloaf. That box turned lima beans into linoleum and pizza into paste. The Big "M" stood for murder, and the victim was supper.

But the nuker was something else that it took me years to recognize. It was my call to arms.

At the grand age of thirteen and a half, I recognized

it was up to me—the girl in the Sex Pistols T-shirt with Janis Joplin hair, who couldn't even make instant coffee—to save my family. I answered the call with a secret missile aimed right for the heart, a little ditty I pull out to this day when the going gets tough. I call it mozzarella.

There they were, sitting in the living room, dull eyes fixed on *Happy Days* reruns, my heartsick family with rumbling stomachs and bored souls. They were so lost, they didn't even know what they were missing.

Just as Mom called us to the table to dine from microwave-safe bowls on a stew-like concoction that might have been noodles, I pounced. Darting behind her, I pulled out hot-from-the-oven (the oven!) pizza bagels studded with mushrooms and—gasp—oregano.

A hush fell over the room. Reluctantly, my brother sniffed at the round, gooey thing, broke off a small piece, and placed it on his tongue.

His eyes grew wide with excitement, and he announced, "This doesn't taste yucky!"

My dad tried one with a begrudging grunt. (Dad grunted his way through about ten years of my childhood, so I'd come to recognize this particular grunt as the "food good" grunt, not the "be quiet or I'll crack you one" grunt.)

My sister grabbed one and started chewing away as she hummed along to one of the endless *Partridge Family* songs playing in her head.

My mom seemed to frown and smile at once.

"There's no nutrition in that," she screeched, but plopped a pizza bagel on her plate all the same.

My life was forever changed.

My father began to ask me strange things like, "Do you mind if I change the channel?" More notably, he used human words, not grunts!

My sister stopped sneaking into my bedroom to steal clean underwear.

My brother began to call me by my name instead of . . . well, nevermind.

From the moment I pulled that first batch of pizza bagels from the oven, I knew that food was magical. Never mind drugs, this was the stuff—a mind-altering mishmash of stimuli that I could meld into every imaginable shape and flavor. I could become a foodie superhero!

For years, my mom's Hungarian recipes, handed down since the Ice Age, were the only things cooked in our home, but I wanted what my friends' moms were making for dinner—pizza, mac and cheese, something a little more "now."

Left to my own artistic wanderings, I came up with mad-scientist dishes like rice pilaf mixed with spaghetti. I gave my creations kooky names like "rice-a-getti" or "meatloaf-aise."

Nobody seemed to mind when I cut up Empire Kosher fried chicken and mixed it with macaroni, margarine, and peas. Try it, but use butter if you're not kosher. Decades later, I have to say this is still pretty tasty, though today I skip the broken-corn-chip topping. That was overkill.

After I turned fourteen and started high school, anything left of my good-girl pretense dissipated in a haze of

Marlboro Lights, marijuana, cheap wine, and chocolate. I became the hostess of numerous after-school soirees.

They were simple affairs. I waited for Mom to leave the house, then my derelict friends would come over and sit on the front porch listening to Led Zeppelin while I concocted a variety of dishes, with one ingredient in common: Snickers bars. It was haute cuisine for teens.

The sight of the sloppy, drooling faces of my somewhat-stoned friends devouring Snickers and Potato Chip Casserole to the tune of "Stairway to Heaven" was as good as it gets.

"Hey man! Rossi is, like, out-of-sight cool, man! She's, like, the best, man!" came the chorus of the gang of high school students who spent more time in detention than they did in class.

My status rocketed from weird, outsider chick to ruler of the planet.

In our family, each kid had jobs. Mine were taking out the garbage and, due to a lifelong habit of looking down when I walked, acting as doo-doo pointer. Neither made me feel truly needed. Then, suddenly, that elusive sensation of being the only one who could provide what everyone wanted was in my grasp, wedged between the kitchen mitts and the platter of cheese ravioli. It was a lesson I would never forget: Power is delicious. And so are pizza bagels.

## Rossi's Teenage Pizza Bagels

*Serves up to 12 people*

**INGREDIENTS**
*12 bagels*
*1 coffee cup of your favorite tomato sauce (When I was
    a kid, I used Ragu.)*
*½ bag (about a pound) grated mozzarella*
*Dried oregano*

**OPTIONAL**
*1 (8 oz.) can mushrooms*

Cut one bagel in half for each family member or stoned
friend present.

Spread your favorite tomato sauce on top of each half.
I always went for jarred marinara, but pizza sauce or
whatever you have will do.

Top with enough grated mozzarella to cover the sauce.

I sprinkled dried oregano on top 'cause I was a fancy
babe. I sometimes topped them with sliced canned
mushrooms. This was years before I knew mushrooms
came any other way.

Lay them in a baking pan and put in the oven at
anywhere from 350 to 400 degrees—350 if, like me, you

prefer soft and cheesy pizza. If you're the crustier type, crank the oven up to 400.

Cook till the cheese is melted and it's as crusty as you like it. About 8–10 minutes should do it.

When I started to cook professionally, I served these as kiddy delights at a bar mitzvah or three. I tried to jazz things up with bell peppers and onions and sautéed shiitake mushrooms on top, but the kids strongly preferred the original teen Rossi recipe. What can I say? Some things are meant to be left simple.

## Snickers and Potato Chip Casserole

*Serves 6 not-stoned teenagers or 2 who are stoned*

**INGREDIENTS**
*2 Snickers bars*
*½ stick sweet butter*
*3 handfuls marshmallows*
*1 bag plain potato chips*

Chop up your Snickers bars into chunks. Cut the butter into pieces. Grease a 9-inch pan or dish (a glass pie plate would do fine) with butter.

Over low heat, melt the butter. Then add the Snickers and marshmallows. Crumble up the potato chips with your hands and then mix the melted Snickers, butter, and marshmallow goop with your crumbled potato chips. Your ratio should be about equal chips to goop.

FYI—go for plain chips, not salt and vinegar or anything like that.

Once you mix, scrape the goop into your buttered pan and smush till it's all in. Top with a smidge more crumbled chips and let cool. When cool, you can cut it into the size pieces you want to devour.

This is so nasty, but lord, nothing tastes better to a teenager.

# Pesach on the Interstate

Cleaning the house in preparation for Passover is an ordeal. You have to pack up all the *treif* (not-kosher-for-Passover food), including the dishes used to serve the treif, scrub the house top to bottom, then actually remove all the packed-up treif and treif-ware.

You can throw away all your food or work a common loophole and "sell" your food to the nearest non-Jewish neighbor for a dollar, then buy it back after Passover. That wasn't a plan that set well with Mom, though, who didn't trust anyone to safeguard a year's worth of food she'd hoarded from all over the county with three-for-one coupon sales.

"Leave my thirty-eight cans of tuna in water . . . with a nonblood relative?" You'd have thought she was talking about the Hope Diamond.

Mom trudged through the annual clean-a-thon for years, working another loophole by declaring that the pantry in our garage, with freezer, fridge, and storage shelves, did not count as part of the house.

"It's an extension, not part of the original structure! The Lord knows this!"

But year after year, her enthusiasm waned. "Major cleaning" had long ago left her vocabulary.

We ate in the kitchen, since the room that we laughably still called "the dining room" had lost its original purpose about a week after we moved in. It was now a two-hundred-square-foot storage room with a folding table on each of its four walls, piled three feet high with items Mom had decided were worth saving: old magazines, four-for-a-dollar batteries, coffee mugs with bank logos on them, shoeboxes filled with coupons, advertisements for sales that ended years before, clothing that had never fit anyone in the family, and the occasional rotting pear.

When we were all together, without the distraction of school or work or personal crisis, we drove each other stark, raving mad. So we hit the road . . . a lot. My dad bought a camper he could wedge onto his yellow Ford pickup, and we began an annual summer trek from Jersey to the Deep South.

For the eight or nine months a year that we weren't traveling, the camper, plucked from the truck like a shell from a hermit crab, sat in our New Jersey backyard on cinder blocks. In our affluent town, the camper cemented our reputation as the white-trash family on the block. Literally. But it came to mean so much more to my mother.

Mom began her Passover sighing a few weeks early the year I turned eleven. She'd look at the twenty loaves of bread and the space in the not-part-of-the-original-structure pantry that could hold maybe a jelly bean and sigh. She'd look at the mountain of dishes piled up near the sink, survey the remaining shelf space in the pantry that might hold a teacup, and sigh. Finally, after throwing herself into a major depression, Mom stepped outside to get some air.

It was there that her eyes fell on the camper. One small room on wheels, a tiny kitchenette, all food items already removed the summer before. It was like a message from the Almighty: "You have suffered too much, dear lady . . . suffer no more!"

One bottle of Pine-Sol and a roll of aluminum foil later, Mom had Passovered the camper.

"Children, we are hitting the road for our seder this year," she announced with glee.

"How's that?" Dad asked, digging in the fridge for his tenth piece of leftover chicken to hold him over for the fifteen minutes till dinner.

"Simple. We just pack up our Passover food and drive!"

So, on a sunny day in April 1975, my sister, brother, dad, mom, and I hit Interstate 95 with enough kosher-for-Passover cans of corned beef hash to feed Michigan.

Keeping Passover was always a challenge, but keeping Passover at truck stops in the South was impossible. Basically, the only thing safe to devour was air, and even that was ill advised at highway truck stops in the seventies.

Mom made all our meals in the camper. Now, let me

explain what this really meant. The bed Mom and Dad slept on doubled as the dining table once the mattress was removed. The only problem was, well, it always smelled like Mom and Dad. No matter what you ate at the table, there was a hint of athlete's foot powder and roll-on deodorant. To further the downscale experience, my dad, well known among his racquetball buddies for going to the men's room just as the check arrived, was a strong advocate of the free campground.

A free campground, for those of you far too classy to know, was not a campground at all, but just a place to park for the night where we wouldn't have to pay. A good twenty-four-hour convenience store didn't mind a loud family from Jersey buying five dollars worth of hair products and then spending the night in the parking lot.

While families wheeled past our camper, pushing carts filled with paper towels and knee socks, Mom prepared the seder plate: roasted bone (Mom substituted one over-cooked hard-boiled egg), sprigs of green (she had found aging celery sticks on sale), horseradish, salt water, and charoseth (a combination of apples, walnuts, and red wine), then matzo, of course.

We sat around the dinette table with our Haggadoth, and my dad led us through the seder.

"Why is this night different from all others?" he read.

"Because on all other nights, we can eat pizza," my brother razzed back.

"Because on all other nights, we could go to a motel instead of this fakaka parking lot," I cried.

"Can I have ten dollars?" asked my sister.

*"Ma nishtanah haly la hazeh mikol halay lot!"* Mom sang so loudly a shopper passing by nearly dropped her twelve pack of Fresca.

When I was fourteen, my parents decided to take us for a more *authentic* seder camping experience. Maybe Dad had developed wanderlust for the great outdoors or a desire to walk outside with his morning cup of instant coffee and not be confronted with a dozen shoppers.

We drove past magical campgrounds in the Carolinas, with snack shops, rolling creeks, inground swimming pools, and recreation rooms, but all these campgrounds had something in common: they were too expensive for Dad. Instead, he opted for the distant campground, the one that didn't spring for flashy billboards, the one he had to ask the toothless guy in the gas station how to find. Dad anointed this campground with his highest praise: "It's a good deal!"

As we entered the grounds, I felt as though we were driving into a gold rush town that had gone bust. A pile of old tires greeted us on the left. On the right, bikers sat around a small fire.

"Cool!" I announced.

"Don't let them see you stare!" Mom shrieked.

We drove a little farther and passed a rusty, old Airstream trailer with two long-haired men out front on folding chairs. A pile of empty Budweiser cans loomed large behind them. One of the men finished his beer and threw the can over his shoulder. It landed with a loud clink on the pile. The other one stood up and saluted as we passed.

Dad found an empty area under a tree that was uphill from the motley crew we'd just driven past. He parked us there.

We helped Mom set up the folding dinette set under the tree. Mom put the seder plate and grape juice on the table, then busied herself heating matzo balls out of a jar and canned chicken broth. Matzo balls out of a jar are a special treat when you're traveling. They remove the need to use public restrooms; two days of them, and you're good for a week. The alternative was something called egg kichel, which is sort of like a ball of cardboard coated with egg wash.

We sat down and began to recite the Passover Seder.

*"Dai, Dai, Dayenu, Dayenu, Dayenu!"*

A fat man wearing a dirty T-shirt that only half covered his hairy stomach walked over.

"Got any ice?"

"No," my father said, instinctively placing his hand on his butter knife.

"We've got egg kichel!" I said, causing my father to grunt his disapproval.

"Sounds nasty," the guy said, scratching his stomach, and walked away.

"Now we enjoy the festive meal!" Mom announced and dragged my sister and me into the camper. First course, constipation soup; entrée, yellow asparagus spears, burned kosher chicken, egg matzo, and pickles. I covered my chicken with ketchup and turned it into a matzo sandwich. The pickle was the garnish.

Dessert was the best part of Passover: chocolate-covered macaroons, jelly slices, chocolate-covered matzo, and flourless almond cake. After devouring enough sugar to jump-start a Chevy, we were then told the most horrible thing a sugared-up kid could hear: "Time to go to bed."

Mom and Dad would turn the dinette table back into their bed, lie down, and start snoring immediately. This left the three of us with no option but to go insane. Lily had wised up long ago and stockpiled romance comic books for these occasions. I wrote poetry about the great loves I had never had, places I had never been. Matt indulged in his favorite pastime: terrorizing his older sisters. He would wait until we got comfortable and then crawl up to the top bunk and try to wipe his nose drippings on us.

Trapped between my parents snoring, my brother's snot, my sister's humming, and the stench of corned beef hash cans festering in the sink, I knew I had to make my escape. I pulled on my toughest jean jacket and snuck out. It was dark, but I found a small flashlight with a bank logo on it in the glove compartment.

I walked down the hill, past the hippie camper and the snoring bikers, my heart beating fast. Then I heard music. It was a guitar strumming and a man's voice singing, soft and sweet. I followed the sound and found a group of young men sitting around a fire, passing around a jug of wine. They smoked cigarettes and flicked the ashes into the fire; one of them smoked a joint. They didn't look much older than me, maybe four or five years, but they seemed decades away from the loudmouthed boys from my freshman year of high school.

One of them spotted me.

"Hey, honey, want some wine?"

I looked around. No parents. No cops. No problem.

"Sure!"

I sat down at the fire and took a swig of sweet, tangy Almaden.

"Where ya from?" the redheaded guy asked in a heavy Southern drawl.

"New Jersey."

"Well, make yourself comfy, Yankee girl!"

It was then that I heard the twigs snap. When I spun around, I saw my sister standing in the starlight. I assumed she would run back and tell Mom and Dad, but instead she walked over and sat down next to me.

"Hi!" was all she said.

Lily and I sat there with the boys, drinking wine and pretending to smoke cigarettes.

The singer, a handsome young man with a faint mustache looked over at me. "You're pretty," he said.

"Thanks!" I said, blushing, and I drank a little more wine.

I could feel the fire warming my face and closed my eyes, listening to him sing, "When I find myself in times of trouble / Mother Mary comes to me . . . "

"This is the best Passover ever," Lily whispered.

I felt the boy next to me put his arm around my back. It felt good against the cold, and I snuggled into it. My sister saw and smiled.

Then I heard it.

"Come over here right now!" came the loud, unmistakable voice of my father.

His hands were in the pockets of his pants as though he were getting ready to pull out some hidden weapon.

"Do you know how old these girls are?" he yelled, and then dragged us both away by our arms.

We assumed we'd get a hearty smack, but instead my dad hung his head in exhaustion and crawled back onto the dinette table.

"We'll talk about this tomorrow," he said.

Lily and I climbed up to the top bunk.

We lay there with our eyes open, staring at the camper ceiling. I was alive with new sensations, the taste of wine lingering in my mouth.

My sister began to sing in a faint whisper, "When I find myself in times of trouble . . . "

I joined in, "Mother Mary comes to me . . . "

The next day, Dad sprung for a Ramada Inn with an inground swimming pool, color TV, and brand new shag carpet.

We left the camper in the parking lot that night.

## Not-Kosher-for-Passover
## Canned Corned Beef Hash Omelets

*Serves 2 people*

I simply cannot find that kosher-for-Passover canned corn beef hash Mom used when we were kids, so let's just say that any can of corned beef hash will do. Forgive me, Mom.

**INGREDIENTS**

*1 (7.5 or 8 oz.) can corned beef hash*
*4 eggs*
*Salt and fresh ground pepper*
*1 drizzle vegetable oil if you're kosher, a plop sweet*
*    butter if you're not*

Dump the can of hash in a pot to heat up.

Meanwhile, mix up 4 eggs and season with salt and pepper. Get a skillet hot, and pour in a tad of veggie oil, then your eggs.

Stir and shimmy, shaking your groove thing to celebrate the Passover miracle until the eggs begin to set, then drop your hash by the spoonful onto one side and fold the omelet over to enclose the hash.

## Manischewitz Spritzer

*Amount depends on how much your friends drink*

This is the perfect accompaniment to your seder meal. Plus you can make extra to share with your campground neighbors. I mean, who doesn't love screw-top wine on the rocks? I know it sounds about as yummy as herring casserole, but in the spirit of a white-trash Passover, try it. It's kinda fun.

**INGREDIENTS**
*1 bottle Manischewitz kosher-for-Passover grape wine*
*1 bottle apple juice*
*1 bottle sparkling water*
*Ice*
*A couple orange slices*

Pour one part Manischewitz wine, one part apple juice, and one part sparkling water over ice. Garnish with an orange slice.

# Jewish Migration

When summer rolled around, it was time for our Jewish migration. Bolting the camper to Dad's pickup, loading it with kids, cutoffs, and enough canned goods to feed Des Moines, we headed down I-95 from South Jersey to North Florida.

My folks said the reason for our pilgrimage was to check on their "real estate," a cluster of rinky-dink bunga-lows in a crappy part of town on what was then the Red-neck Riviera: Panama City, Florida. The real reason we hit the road the day after school let out was neither prop-erty inspection nor wanderlust, but the need to escape being at home together all summer.

I don't know if I-95 really was one long white line lead-ing to the Deep South like I picture it. Maybe a few twists and turns happened while I was sleeping. I was indulging in my favorite activity: daydreaming.

I daydreamed from Jersey through Delaware and Maryland every June. They were the states that seemed the most forgettable to me then, and, well, now. In my daydreams I was one of two things: a hero or a rock star.

As a hero, I saved kids at school from a sniper attack by sneaking up behind the gunman and hitting him with a bottle. I was stuck on the bottle-hitting thing, but I tried it out on a sidewalk once, and they really don't break as easily as they do in the movies.

As a rock star, I was on stage in front of my screaming, adoring fans, belting out a song that would make Janis Joplin jealous.

I never dreamed about being a pudgy thirteen-year-old in the early days of puberty.

Once past Virginia, I started taking reality breaks from my daydreaming. I counted the rows of tobacco in the fields, read the billboards for fireworks and pecan pie, and stayed alert for any chance to pull into a roadside diner with a Southern breakfast special.

In 1977 a breakfast special at a Southern highway diner was worth the whole trip. I am talking about coffee with as many refills as you want, buttermilk biscuits and homemade jam, sweet creamy butter and gravy, two eggs so slick and greasy they'd slide right off the plate if you didn't keep it completely level. Then came the grits, hash browns, and toast.

All this was served to you for ninety-nine cents by a waitress in a blue uniform with a lace apron named Blanche or May or Charlene, who wore streaks of frosty green eye shadow and set her hair up into a bouffant kept in place by a white doily in the shape of a tiara.

Inside the camper, my sister and I slept on the top bed, placing us in the overhang on the roof of the Ford, the most glamorous spot in the camper during cool weather.

*My mother dragging my sister and me in the Nova to the kosher butcher (1978).*

But in the heat of summer, we coveted my brother's spot.

His single bed lay against "the hole," the crawlway from the camper into the front seat of the Ford, where my parents blasted the air-conditioning until frost formed on the windows.

They'd been too cheap to get a camper that had AC venting into it, so we all fought over the hole, and sometimes, when it hit ninety or above, we would crawl through the hole and slither snakelike between my parents. However, no amount of wondrous air-conditioning was enough of a reward for being the Oreo filling to my folks.

My dad pretty much spent the ride grunting, eating apples, and trying desperately to get my mother to stop talking. He's the only person I ever met who could say "shut up" as one syllable: "shuuuuuup!"

Unfazed, Mom would babble on about a never-ending abundance of things none of us gave a hoot about.

She worried about the old lady she'd just had a heart-warming conversation with in the checkout line of the Piggly Wiggly supermarket. "Oh, I hope her back feels better soon!"

She worried a lot about the Jews. "It can happen again, I tell you! Hitlers are born every day!"

She worried about whether the collection of coupons she was hoarding in her purse had expired.

She had a stream-of-consciousness style. Details of the strangers with whom she'd just become best friends gave way to a discourse about the terrible thing that was happening to the Jews this week, and that in turn led to a barrage of the two-for-one sales we were about to miss. After approximately fifteen minutes of Mom torture, we slithered from the cool front seat back to the sauna on wheels.

One would think that bedtime would be a relief from Mom's chatter. Thankfully, she didn't talk in her sleep, but that doesn't mean she was quiet. Nighttime, when we parked for what was supposed to be sleep, my mother let out strange, gastric noises. In the few moments when something didn't sound like it was erupting from her, my father snored, my sister hummed, or my brother wheezed. This almost indescribable combination of noises made up the Ross Family Symphony, and there was just no sleeping through it.

The entire camper was about the size of my small bedroom at home, and here my family of five sweltered the night away.

I never slept when we parked.

But on extra hot nights, my sister, brother, and I would begin our motel whine a good two hours before sleep time: "Motel, motel, motel with pool, motel," and if it was hot enough and we whined long enough, it usually worked.

Now, my dad liked a good swimming pool, color TV, and AC as much as we did, but he and my mom always held out until the last possible second, when we were almost too tired to enjoy these luxuries, because of a notion they fostered that if you pulled into a motel late enough and there were still rooms free and you paid in cash, you could almost always get one at half-price.

I never was able to convince them that even though

this was usually true, if all you did was pass out without using the pool, the TV, or the ice machine and were too tired to even roll around in the shag rug or try ripping off the candy machine, then who cared if it was half-price? In Kidland, this was a lousy deal.

# Hot Dog Antipasto Salad

*Serves 4 to 6 people*

When we camped, the first things on the grill were Hebrew National hot dogs, mostly because they cooked fast and could shut up our kvetching family. Mom would throw enough dogs on the grill to feed half the Jews in Brooklyn.

I think it was Mom's revenge for spending the money on a motel, but when we did get to stay in one, we were often treated to culinary delights like cut-up wrinkle-dog and mustard sandwiches. "What? It's just like bologna," she would scream.

**INGREDIENTS**

*4 leftover cooked hot dogs, sliced*
*½ red onion, minced*
*1 cucumber, sliced or diced*
*4 plum tomatoes, diced*
*2 sticks of celery, sliced*
*1 (7 oz.) jar artichoke hearts*
*1 coffee cup pepperoncini*
*1 (6 oz.) jar pimientos*
*3 shots Italian dressing*
*1 head iceberg, romaine, or Boston lettuce*
*½ (8 oz.) jar olives*

**OPTIONAL**

*1 heaping handful provolone cheese, diced*

So here's how it goes. Take day-old cooked and chilled hot dogs, slice them up, and toss them with minced red onion, sliced or diced cucumber, diced plum tomatoes, thinly sliced celery, and a couple of fun antipasto fixings. Pick your favorites. I like artichoke hearts, pepperoncini, or sliced pimientos. Mix the whole shebang in your favorite Italian dressing, and pour it over a bed of lettuce.

Garnish with sliced olives—almost any kind will do. If you're not kosher, add a heaping handful of diced provolone cheese.

If you have a sense of humor, you can make croutons out of any leftover hot dog buns. Slice 'em or cube 'em up, toss in olive oil, salt, and pepper, then toast in the oven at 350 degrees until nice and crunchy. Sprinkle them over your salad and congratulate yourself for such a thematic dish.

# The Day Elvis Died

The day Elvis died, I was trapped by my mother in a plus-size clothing store in Southern Georgia.

We were dragging a little that day, worn out from a motel-less night parked at a truck stop just a mile or so past a full-service Ramada Inn—so close and yet so far. Just when I didn't think life could get any worse, my mother dragged me and my sister to a bargain clothing store for big women, while my brother and father did man things like check the truck's oil and battery.

Not one to miss a bargain, Mom had made this particular clothing store a regular stop on the aforementioned annual Jewish migration.

Inside were racks and racks of brightly colored, extra-loose cotton dresses. Living in Southern Georgia necessitated clothes that fell off your body, not stuck to it. I could see the advantage.

I was feeling really uncomfortable about the strange things that were happening to my body, and I imagined hiding inside one of the large cotton housedresses, disap-

pearing in the waves of soft yellow, pink, and magenta . . .
feeling weightless and invisible.

The store was filled with a dozen or so large Southern women, black and white, dragging their chubby
kids around. "Chubby" was the polite term back then.
If "chubby" still hurt your feelings, there was always
"husky," which sounded almost like a compliment.

I was husky, said my mother.

My sister—the skinny one—had abandoned the fat-
lady ship immediately and was sitting on the floor in the
group changing room reading romance comic books and
pretending not to watch the fat moms undress, leaving
me at the mercy of my mother's fashion sense.

"How about a nice pink polka-dot dress for back to
school?" she offered, in complete denial of the fact that
the only thing I hated more than dresses was polka dots.

Every fifteen minutes or so, a high-pitched, overly
feminine voice would come out of the loudspeaker,
which was really not necessary in the tiny store. The voice
would announce things like, "Ladies . . . if you'll head on
over to aisle twooooo, there's a half-off sale on slips, and
they'rrrre reeeel purteeeee!"

Then the fat moms would stampede to aisle two, leaving us chubby and husky kids behind on the rumbling
floor.

I was hiding behind a rack of bumblebee-yellow housedresses, watching my mom go into her shopping trance,
when the crackling of the speaker came on for the last
time.

Crackle crackle . . . "Laaaadiesssssssss . . . Lord help us. Eeeellllllviiiisss is deaddddd! Heeee's deadddddddd!" followed by a kind of muffled, whimpering sound, and then the microphone clicked off.

Time froze, as it does in the movies when something really terrible has happened, and I turned and stared at all those faces in suspended animation. Shock, disbelief, silence. Then . . . like a surge coming up from way down under, a giant simultaneous wail.

"OOOOOOOOOH NOOOOOOOOOOOOOOOOO! Lord . . . Noooooooo!"

The fat ladies started clutching at their breasts, crying and asking the Lord to make it not so, and all the children came running to their moms screaming, "Mama, Mama, what's wrong?"

Racks of pantsuits marked "As Is" spilled across the floor like a sea of 2-D secretaries, and one of the chubby kids dove under them, scared and blinking.

It was pure pandemonium.

In the middle of it all, amid pastels flying, babies screaming, shrieking mothers' breasts heaving, stood my northern Jewish mom, looking around at all of them, grasping the moment, listening to the eerie sounds of fat-lady despair.

Then she got a faraway look in her eyes, as though she was remembering something from too many years ago. She sat down among the racks of extra-wide shoes and started to cry.

Long after the Southern moms had composed themselves and reapplied their powder and eye shadow, my mother sat in that chair and cried.

I didn't understand, but I tried to comfort her by rubbing her shoulder and holding one of her hands between mine.

"Mommy," I whispered, ". . . I didn't know you liked Elvis so much."

Mom looked me in the eye for the longest two seconds I have ever experienced, scrunched up her nose in that way she did whenever something confused her, and said, "Why? Did something happen to Elvis?"

## Eggs I'd Cook for Elvis

*Serves 2 to 4 mortals or 1 rock 'n' roll legend with a hearty appetite*

**INGREDIENTS**
*6 eggs, beaten*
*Salt and fresh ground pepper*
*2 heaping plops sweet butter*
*1 handful white onion, minced*
*1 handful bell pepper, diced*
*1 heaping handful breakfast sausage (maybe 4 links),*
*    sliced or diced*

**OPTIONAL**
*4 cheese slices*

Beat 6 eggs in a bowl and season to your liking with salt and pepper.

Melt 2 heaping plops of sweet butter in an ovenproof skillet. After the butter melts and foams, add one handful of minced onion and a handful of diced bell pepper.

Cook this for a couple of minutes, then throw in a handful of any kind of sliced or diced sausage. You can try breakfast sausage, vegetarian sausage, or chicken sausage, whatever floats your boat.

Sauté your concoction until the sausage looks pretty well cooked, then turn up the heat a little and pour in the eggs. The trick at this point is to keep stirring (preferably with a wooden spoon) until the eggs begin to set. That's how you get that nice, fluffy omelet look.

Now here's the best part: stick the whole thing in the oven at about 400 degrees, and when it puffs up and starts to brown, it's ready! Easy and breezy, like a plus-size sundress.

To serve, cut into four wedges, or one (for the King).

If you'd like to remember Elvis by adding a few more calories, you can give your breakfast a nice low-rent touch by throwing some Velveeta cheese on top just before you stick the eggs in the oven. Those individually wrapped American cheese slices work, too, but if you use something fancy, like cheddar or Swiss, the eggs will taste too uptown and you'll have to change clothes.

## Kosher Elvis Sandwich

*Serves 2 people*

As a kid, and really as a grown-up, too, two of my great loves were peanut butter and bananas, so it didn't take me long to start making peanut butter and banana sandwiches. Years later, I learned that Elvis, who did not keep kosher, had a favorite sandwich that included peanut butter, bacon, and bananas. So in honor of the King, and my mother, I have created a kosher version.

### INGREDIENTS
*4 slices white bread*
*1 heaping plop peanut butter*
*1 banana, sliced*
*4 slices cooked kosher beef bacon or beef fry strips*
*1 plop kosher margarine or butter*

Start out with 4 slices of white bread, 'cause you might as well make two. They are too good not to share, and you might just want both.

Spread peanut butter on the top and bottom of 2 pieces of bread and cover with sliced bananas. Then top with cooked kosher beef bacon or cooked kosher beef fry strips. Cover with the other slices of bread.

At this point you could eat the sandwich, and it would be fabulous, but to really honor the big guy, spread some kosher margarine on the outside of the bread slices and fry that hound dog in a skillet until the outside is nice and brown and toasty. Should only take a few minutes.

Cut each sandwich in half, and enjoy. Wow, life does not get better than this.

# Suicide Supper

When I was growing up, a family supper meant gathering on metal folding chairs with plastic cushions, part of the deluxe dinette set Mom bought at the Grant's going-out-of-business sale.

She'd throw down a plastic tablecloth that met her "wonderful" test for kitchen items, meaning it could be wiped with a sponge.

The plastic "cloth" she favored was too thick to fold, so the four inches that overlapped the tables stuck straight out, keeping us an additional four inches from our supper, not that I minded. Another four inches from my family was fine with me.

On the wonderful, spongeable cloth were bright, seventies flowers that were the backdrop to my childhood. My memories are paved in fuchsia and paisley.

Mom always served kosher roast chicken. She informed us, despite our requests for a traditional holiday meal, that none of us liked turkey, and that's why.

I actually liked turkey, or liked the idea of it, anyway. I'd only tried it once, in a sandwich slathered with deli mustard, not quite the same as a Thanksgiving roast slathered in gravy. I'd begun romanticizing things I deemed exotic, like holiday meals that included an actual holiday dish.

As we were called to the dinner table, I would have a flash of my fantasy: a roaring fire, the smell of melting butter on hot biscuits, a table set with shiny silverware, china, and glasses.

When we were kids, the table was set with Dixie Riddle Cups. They provided the entertainment while we waited for our meal. We would spin the waxy paper cups around in our hands and read the riddle and answer on the cup.

"What family drinks diet soda out of paper cups, while other families have hot cider from mugs and wine from glasses?" Answer: mine.

Mom had a little rule, anything that took longer than two hours to defrost was rejected. Defrosting a kosher turkey? Never gonna happen.

The kosher chicken was almost always accompanied by asparagus out of the can. I was sixteen before I learned that asparagus came any other way and that its natural color was, in fact, green.

Salad was always the same: iceberg lettuce, no dressing, 'cause dressing is, you know, weird. On the salad would be a pile of raw onions and slabs of tomatoes cut so thick, you could dislocate your jaw.

Sis always went for the onions. She discovered at the age of six that if she bit into a raw onion, ate it, and appeared to like it, it would bring horror and shock to those around her. For this reason, she forced herself to adore raw onions and ate them ever after. That is, of course, until she started dating.

Mom was a double entrée kind of lady, so the chicken was usually accompanied by what she called beef but what was, in fact, a hunk of sirloin cooked for so long that one had to scrape off burned charcoal before eating it. The alternative to charcoal cow briquettes was Mom's beef stew, cooked so long and slow that teeth were not required to eat it. It was tasty but lost its appeal when slopped into a Styrofoam bowl.

When we complained, Mom always said the same thing, "Charcoal is good for you! I do this because I care!"

We did the only thing one could do when it was time to devour a piece of scorched cardboard: we covered it with ketchup from a bowl of McDonald's packets that Mom had pilfered.

The meal was paired with another family delight Mom referred to as "ducky bread."

Some of the bakeries along the Jersey Shore would sell day-old bread in garbage bags for a dollar. The bread was meant to be duck food, of course, but nonetheless, garbage bags filled with eight to ten loaves of bread would find their way to our freezer and our dinner table.

Once when I was six, a goose chased me three blocks. To this day, I'm convinced he knew we were the ones eating all his bread.

We had a holiday food once: canned cranberry sauce. It sat there, this red, can-shaped thing, wiggling almost imperceptibly if any of us moved. I had nightmares that the red cylinder was chasing me. I ran screaming, and it just Slinky-ed along behind me . . . bong, bong, bong . . .

Our family suppers were never just about the food. The real main dish was guilt. Each platter was garnished with a sermon about how long my mom had suffered to make it, or how far she had to travel to find kosher meat, or all the things she didn't do today and yesterday because she was too busy, you know, opening the cans. I didn't mention that she rarely even did that much, once she discovered the microwave.

After the audience was seated, the Ross Family Symphony began. Our dinner overture was epic. My father's gigantic bites created huge sucking sounds. Dad could down a meal in three swallows and ask for seconds before I was halfway into my sirloin beef jerky. It was, in fact, these sucking noises that let us know my father was actually at the dinner table. The man spoke about twice a week. Wordless, otherworldly songs came from my brother, who sang as he played with his food. The chorus from my sister, who just stared at her food and asked for money, included, "The new Barbie is out!" or "I can't go to school without frosted lipstick!" Mom played bass, expelling Mom-normous amounts of gas, with an uncanny ability to do so just as I took a mouthful of food.

"Mom!" we would yell, shoving Burger King napkins into our noses.

"Leave me alone; I have a condition!" she would respond.

After satisfying herself that she had ruined any chance of us tasting what little flavor remained in our overprocessed, overcooked meal, she would relax. This was the signal for the family symphony to begin the second movement: Child-Lecturing in B-Flat. "Would it kill you to help your mother once in a while?" and "When I was your age, I supported my parents, working two jobs and going to school!" I was perhaps the only quiet member of the orchestra, but then my job was always to be the observer.

One year, my parents did something unheard of in my family: they invited a guest to dinner. It was Thanksgiving, and our next-door neighbor, an elderly man we kids called Mr. T., came to supper.

Mr. T. was happy at first, thinking that a meal with a real family was much better than the one he usually attended at his church. Shortly thereafter, he assumed that dazed look reserved for those driving by a really bad traffic accident.

Maybe the plastic silverware got to him. It might have been the Entenmann's turkey cake Mom got on special because someone sat on it. He left early, saying something about a job he had to do, and never dined with us again. The man had options.

I knew in an instant that he knew what I'd been trying to hide for years, the reason I always met my school friends at their houses—I lived in an insane asylum.

As the observer, I considered myself then, as I do today, the family anthropologist.

My mission, like that of all great historians and Andean plane crash survivors, was simple: I had to survive at all costs to tell the story and, you know, become a caterer.

*Ill-fated family supper with Mr. T., my mom, dad, sister,*
*and two boys my sister dragged in from the street (1979).*

# Big Ol' Pot of Beef Stew

*Serves 5 to 8 people*

**INGREDIENTS**
*2 lbs. stew beef*
*Salt and fresh ground pepper*
*1 shot olive oil*
*2 heaping handfuls white onion, chopped*
*2 carrots, peeled and chopped*
*2 celery sticks, sliced*
*1 handful each fresh thyme, fresh oregano, fresh sage*
*4 coffee cups beef stock*
*1 glass red wine*
*1 (16 oz.) can tomatoes*
*5 potatoes, diced*
*1 handful fresh parsley, chopped*

**OPTIONAL**
*1 loaf crusty bread*

Buy stew meat, which should come already cut up into cubes. Might as well buy 2 lbs. because stew gets better every time you reheat it.

Season the family-dinner-hell out of your beef with salt and fresh ground pepper, then get a big, deep skillet or a Dutch oven or any heavy-duty deep pot with a thick bottom. Throw in a shot of olive oil and crank up the heat, then brown the beef nicely on both sides.

Take meat out of the pot. Then in the same pot throw in your veggies: 2 heaping handfuls each of chopped white onion, chopped carrots, and chopped celery.

Sauté your veggies until they are soft and have color on the edges. Add wine and reduce until you don't smell the alcohol, then add your beef stock and tomatoes. You can add seasoning: salt and pepper, thyme, oregano, or sage—whatever you like.

Bring it all to a boil and throw your meat back in.

Lower to a simmer, cover, and cook for an hour. Throw in your potatoes and cook for another half hour or until meat is very soft.

Adjust your seasoning with some more salt and pepper.

Just before serving, add fresh parsley.

Add a big hunk of crusty bread to this, and you've got a feast.

# A Decent Iceberg Lettuce Salad

*Serves 2 to 4 people*

I'm not an iceberg fan of any kind—what icebergs did to the *Titanic*, they did to salad, but folks love this stuff and so do moms. Your best shot is a wedge salad, and I'm here to help.

**INGREDIENTS**
*1 head iceberg lettuce*
*1 heaping plop crumbled blue cheese*
*1 plop mayonnaise*
*1 drizzle balsamic vinegar*
*1 shot olive oil*
*Salt and fresh ground pepper*
*Croutons, any kind*

**OPTIONAL**
*A few strips of bacon*

Wash an iceberg head and discard the crappy outer leaves.

Cut into big wedges (maybe you'll get eight to a head) and put a wedge on each plate you're serving.

Make a sauce out of crumbled blue cheese, mayo, balsamic vinegar, olive oil, and salt and pepper to your liking. Pour over your wedge and serve with a nice big crouton.

We were kosher, so no bacon, dears, but for you, oy vey, bacon away!

# The Exodus

The summer after eighth grade, everything changed. I had spent my last two years of grammar school navigating an excruciating burst of puberty that bestowed on me, to my horror, the largest breasts in school. I buried nature's well-meant extravagance under layers of clothes, and even in hot weather, pulled baggy sweaters over button-downs over T-shirts. And since my mother had neglected to teach her children that puberty meant you needed to start wearing deodorant, I also began to stink.

I'd been a fairly happy fat kid in sixth grade, but in the seventh and eighth grade I spent most of my time hiding in the back of class hoping the bullies wouldn't pick on me. Well, not too much anyway.

Then Sonya Simone moved to town. She was everything for which the preppy little town of Rumson, New Jersey, was unprepared. She was a New Yorker, shopped in exotic places in Manhattan like Fiorucci, wore tight jeans with wide belts, didn't seem to care what anyone thought of her, and was the first girl I'd ever met who wore pumps. She wasn't the prettiest girl in school, or the richest, but she had something better: parents who traveled and left her the house with no chaperone. Within weeks of moving to town, Sonya became queen of the Saturday-night house party.

Her popularity escalated, as every kid who was anyone wanted to go to her bashes, and for some reason, she decided that I should be her friend, too. My mother insisted on buying us horrendous, secondhand clothes. I was frumpy, awkward, rank, and looked like the Michelin Man with all those layers. Some of the bullies in school had taken to mooing when I walked by. But Sonya saw something interesting and took me under her wing.

After all, we were both artists. The obsessive doodling that had satiated my nervous energy throughout grammar school had morphed into large paintings of movie stars and rock stars. Sonya said my rather bad portraits were avant-garde. I'd never heard that term before.

Her belief in me made me a bit braver. Something inside opened its blinking eyes and woke up. That summer, when my folks took my sister, brother, and me to Miami Beach, I peeled off all those sweaty layers and stepped onto the beach in a bathing suit. It wasn't a bikini, yet, but it was a pretty sexy one-piece for a fourteen-year-old.

Needless to say, boys noticed. Grown men, too. The sun turned my skin caramel and my hair blonder, and for the first time, I started to feel beautiful.

I met a handsome twenty-two-year-old Pensacola waterskiing champion who thought I was seventeen. We kissed for hours on the moonlit beach, and my heart felt like it was doing flip-flops.

I learned a lot that summer: how to smoke cigarettes, how to drink beer, how to French kiss, how to roll joints and smoke them, and how to do something I hadn't done since I was a kid—smile.

The freshman who stepped into Rumson-Fair Haven Regional High School that fall was a cross between Janis Joplin and Axl Rose. My hair was wild. I was wearing worn Levi's, a black Rolling Stones T-shirt, and a leather strand around my neck, from which hung a roach clip. I had a pack of Marlboro Lights in my bag and a pint of Hiram Walker Blackberry Brandy in my hip pocket. Kids who'd gone to school with the shy, dowdy "moo" girl didn't even know who I was, which was just as well. The girl I used to be was dead; Rossi, the badass rocker chick, was born!

My freshman and sophomore years were a mad dash to catch up on all the joy I'd missed, but I admit that I also enjoyed a little revenge. I took delight in using my new-found social status as a renegade "cool girl" to turn my admirers against the bullies whom I'd endured in grammar school. I championed the underdogs, as Sonya had done for me, and made the moo-ers run for cover.

I had friends of all ages, was invited to parties every day, and probably would have considered this era of my life the happiest, were it not for one little problem: my parents.

However miserable I'd been in grammar school, I'd been a straight A student. I didn't talk back to my parents, and when I didn't agree with them, I suffered in silence.

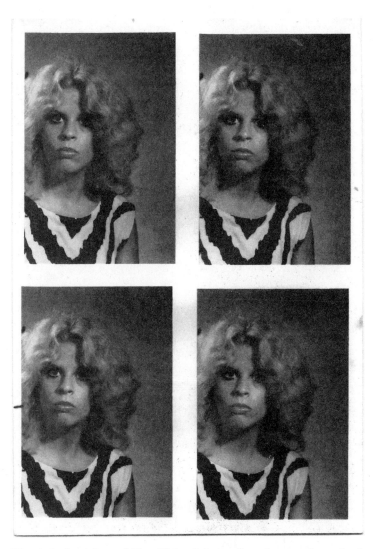

*"Don't fuck with me fellas. This ain't my first time at the rodeo."*
—*Joan Crawford*

But, finally free after two years of being bullied, my suffering-in-silence days were over. I let my parents know exactly what I thought of their double standards: allowing my little brother, who had no interest in leaving my mother's side, to stay out all night if he wanted to and do anything with girls he could get away with, because "the rules are different for boys."

Meanwhile, my sister and I were not allowed out after 10:00 p.m., were not allowed to go to R-rated movies, were not allowed to date anyone but Jewish boys (and then, only with a chaperone), were not allowed to curse or wear revealing clothes, and were strongly discouraged from having any Christian friends whatsoever.

My sister rebelled by wearing enough makeup to pass for a Times Square hooker. She mostly stayed in her room, reading romance novels and banging rather badly on a guitar. I raged against the prison I felt I was in. I dyed my hair pink, put on leather jackets, got in trouble in school, drank, smoked, painted fairly bad portraits of Jim Morrison, and made a point to date just about anyone who wasn't Jewish—bonus points if they weren't male or white.

Our family fights became legendary in my small town. My mother would scream and cry, pound on her chest, and ask the Lord to help her with her crazy daughter. My father would shout and slam doors and dole out harsh sentences on a regular basis. "You are grounded!" became as common as "Pass the bagels." I would sit in the middle of the chaos, arms crossed, yelling dramatic teen pronouncements like, "I don't have to die to go to hell. Because I'm in hell right now!"

Some of the kids I hung around with dropped out and got their GEDs, but I wanted my diploma. I had already decided that I wanted to be an artist when I grew up, not a doctor, lawyer, or any career that required college. But getting that piece of paper still meant something to me, if only so that I could burn it.

So in my junior year I enrolled in a program that let me graduate a year early by doubling my classes and going to summer school. My parents thought I was eager to start art classes in community college, but the truth is I was planning to run away from home, two seconds after graduation.

I'd had my bags packed for a month and my buddy Doug on alert to come over in his huge, old, beat-up Chevy the moment I dialed him and said, "Escape!"

I'd run away from home before, and my folks had always tracked me down. It wasn't hard; I was at one of my burnout pal's houses.

This was different. I'd been planning my escape for a year, working odd jobs to save runaway money. I was going to disappear proper.

The trick was to get thrown out of the house, not just run away. I figured that way they wouldn't come looking for me.

I smoked cigarettes in the house, let the smell of marijuana waft down the stairs, turned up my stereo, blasting Pink Floyd: "We don't need no education / We don't need no thought control!" My other high-volume anthem was Pat Benatar's "Hell Is for Children."

But it was Sonya's mother who actually aced the deal. After years of being corrupted by Sonya, who had taught me how to do everything from smoking from a bong to snorting Dexatrim, Sonya's mom called my mother to say she thought I was corrupting her younger daughter, Sarah, who had become my best friend in the last two years. We were practically inseparable.

"Your daughter is a lesbian!" Sonya's mom shrieked to my horrified mother.

When I got home that night, after an evening of bong hits in Piping Rock Memorial Park, my parents were standing on the front lawn, arms crossed, scowling. The resulting scream-a-thon ended in my father's announcement: "We're going grocery shopping; when we come home, you'd better be ready to obey our rules, which are going to be ten times tougher, or don't be here!"

"You'll see how well I do!" I yelled back, filled with fury.

The moment their Volaré turned the corner, I called Doug.

I filled the trunk with weeks of frozen TV dinners and tossed my packed bags into the backseat. Doug checked me in to a cheap motel on the Sea Bright shore, and off we went on a weeklong adventure.

It was fun, of course, hopping from party to party. I watched as my friends from high school called their folks, making excuses, and left by midnight, but *I* didn't have to go home ever again. After years of feeling like I was in prison, the freedom was almost maddening.

After two weeks of fun, I'd made a scary dent in my $3,000 savings, so I checked out of the semidecent Sea Bright motel and into a lower-rent place in Long Branch famous for its crime rate. Mostly prostitutes and truckers slept there, but it was seventy a week, just across the street from the ocean, and the manager didn't ask for ID. Good thing, since I was sixteen. Doug left me a hot plate he had swiped from his mother. Sometimes I would cook a gourmet supper of pasta with canned peas (stolen from Mom) and chopped up hot dogs.

Things were okay for a while, but as summer ended, the Long Branch Amusement Pier began to quiet down. My friends went back to high school, the crowds dispersed, and the weather turned from glorious sunshine to drizzly rain, haze, and dampness. I had $500 left and counted pennies to buy the egg roll and coffee special at the local bar and grill. It cost ninety-nine cents, and I never left the penny. I was going to have to find a job without showing ID. This left me a few options: A. Dancing at the Tideaway Rock Lounge, where you didn't have to take off your bikini; B. Selling pot for local dealers; C. Mooching money off all my friends until the friendships dried up; D. I had no friggin' idea!

I don't know what the occasion was—it may have been my birthday, may have been that I was just feeling too alone—but I decided to throw a party in my motel room. I invited Sarah, my fifteen-year-old favorite person in the world, a few high school pals, and, for some reason I cannot explain to this day, a half-dozen sailors.

I'm guessing the motel manager had had just about

enough of the stream of teenagers spending the night in his motel. Criminals, hookers, truckers, serial-killer wannabes were all fine, but teenagers? Too dangerous.

He called the cops.

# Hot Plate Hebrew Nationals and Pasta

*Serves 2 to 4 people*

### INGREDIENTS

*3 hot dogs or ¹/₃ a salami or bologna, cut into bite-size*
    *pieces*
*1 (8 oz.) can tomato sauce*
*1 (8 oz.) can peas*
*Salt and fresh ground pepper*
*1 pinch dried oregano*
*1 lb. dry pasta, any kind*

### OPTIONAL

*1 (8 oz.) can beans, any kind*

Throw bite-size pieces of hot dogs, salami, or bologna in a skillet and fry till brown. Then add a can of tomato sauce, a can of peas, and season with pepper. You probably won't need salt with all that cured meat, but add a pinch if you want, then add a pinch of oregano.

Boil and drain your fave pasta and pour sauce over pasta.

You can also use canned beans of almost any kind instead of peas for this "franks and beans meets spaghetti" gastronomic meltdown.

## White Trash but Keepin' It Kosher Tuna and Macaroni Salad

*Serves 2 teenagers or 4 grown-ups*

**INGREDIENTS**
*1 lb. macaroni*
*1 coffee cup mayonnaise*
*1 large can tuna*
*½ red onion, diced*
*2 celery stalks, diced*
*1 large kosher dill pickle, chopped*
*1 (8 oz.) can peas*
*1 pinch salt and fresh ground pepper*

Boil one box of macaroni and drain. Cool off under cold water then drain again.

Combine mayo, tuna, red onion, celery, pickle, peas, and salt and pepper. Mix it all up and enjoy.

# Rebbe-Land USA

After the cops raided my teens-and-sailors party, landing me in the backseat of my parents' Volaré, it was clear to my mom that her house could not contain this particular nice Jewish girl turned wild child.

I often wonder what would have happened if Mom had not read about a young rabbi who took in and reformed wild Jewish kids in one of her Jewish publications and then decided that a massive dose of Judaism was just what the doctor ordered.

And so on a rainy afternoon, my parents plopped me and my luggage in the car and carted me off to the Lubavitch Hasidic community in Brooklyn. It was like Mars . . . with matzo balls.

All I had from my Long Branch days were three hundred bucks and the emerging realization that being a minor with pink hair made me highly unemployable. I decided to play nice. Once my funds were replenished and I learned how to get to New York City, I'd make my escape. In the meantime, I allowed the rabbi's family to believe that they might bring me around.

They allowed me a spot on the living room couch plus two hot meals a day, in exchange for following a couple of simple rules: I would attend Hebrew classes at least three days a week and show respect for the Sabbath from sundown Friday until sundown Saturday. Got it.

My status as an oh-so-lost child of Israel made me immediately popular in the hood. Hasidic moms fought over who would have me at their house for Shabbas. In addition to opportunities to bring me into the fold, I offered the "lifers" amusing and astounding stories of the outside world.

"Tell us more of this thing called slam dancing!" they would coo. I'm convinced that the person who actually got me to be *frum* (devout) would get a big trophy or a toaster oven or something. That's how hard they tried.

"Slovah," they would say (using my Yiddish name), "you will learn to feel free in this community because your heart will be elevated all the time." I didn't feel very elevated, having gained five pounds eating schnitzel, strudel, kugel, and all those other dishes that ended with "el."

Having never lived in New York City, I didn't realize at first how dangerous Crown Heights was. The Hasids provided their own protection. They armed themselves with baseball bats and formed a "civilian patrol," driving around the neighborhood in station wagons. If someone was being attacked, they would teach the assailants a lesson straight from the Bible: Thou Shalt Not Mug!

I quickly learned that it was best to run the two blocks from the subway station to the Hasid-protected zone. It was a good way to burn off the new weight, anyway.

The rabbi's wife used to cart me to the synagogue on Friday nights to listen to the rebbe, the famous Rabbi Schneerson. I liked the rebbe almost immediately and delighted in the irony that he looked exactly like Santa Claus.

But being shoved into the women's tower of the synagogue outraged me. I could see the men dancing freely in the open-air main floor below while I was herded in with hundreds of women, seated (if you could find a seat) on hard wooden bleachers. I left each service with a need for an Epsom salt bath and an urge to start a women's rights march.

I wondered out loud why the men were not shut in the tower and the women dancing below. The horrified women would hiss, "Shhhh!"

Feminism was not popular in shul.

To be *tzniut* (modest), I was told not to sing when men were present, as the sensual voice of a woman might distract them from prayer. (Clearly, no one had heard me sing.)

I was asked to cover myself above the elbows and from the knees up and the collarbone down and never to wear pants. It was assumed that I would learn the customs, go to shul, and marry a man I would not know but would grow to love. I was then expected to have somewhere between six and twelve children and never have physical contact with a man, not even a handshake, except for my husband and my sons for the rest of my life.

I found this less than amusing.

But I liked the rebbe. It was clear why he was a living

legend. His soft, brilliant eyes peering out from that mass of white fur beckoned to me. I knew right then and there that I would probably tell my grandchildren about him as they sat with captivated awe, or, well, at least somebody's grandchildren. I wasn't exactly on a crash course to motherhood.

My first *Farbrengen* (Rebbe's speech) came just before the High Holy Days. The rebbe spoke in Yiddish, which was then interpreted and piped through speakers hanging from the ceilings. As the building, known as 770, became overstuffed with awestruck followers, the Hasidim would gather outside by the hundreds around additional speakers. I had been lucky enough to get smushed inside before the rush.

The rebbe's speech focused mostly on children and how they were the future. He dreamed of Jewish children carrying a message of unity and peace for generations.

A single word from him sent shudders through the masses that gathered inside 770, screams from the street outside, followed by a distant purr from the homes along Eastern Parkway tuned in to the live radio broadcast. Even to a jaded teenage girl, his message was electric.

After a month of sleeping on a couch, I used the few hundred dollars my parents sent me to move out of the rabbi's home, with his permission of course, and into a large apartment with three other young women. Finally, after what seemed like a decade, I had my own room. I can still remember the ecstasy of that sound—the rub and click as my bedroom door shut behind me.

We were social girls, bent on finding a way to have fun without hearing about it from the elders. On Sunday nights, our flat filled with just-past-adolescence women, some in the first stages of the *Shidduch* (arranged marriage), most still missing blue jeans and Christian boys. We would bust out from our chains, sing loudly and out of tune with the radio, and laugh as we drank horribly sweet kosher wine from coffee cups.

When we weren't in our apartment, we gathered at the kosher pizza shop and smoked cigarettes, comparing our rage at the expectations of submission and double standards. "Why must I marry someone I don't even know?" asked Anya, a British girl raised in Israel. "I want to marry for love, not the hope of love."

I spent hours in a booth at the kosher pizza place, nibbling on pizza, falafel, and hummus (which sounds disgusting but somehow worked), with my Parisian roomie Fagee and Tova, a *baal t'shuvah* woman (a Jew who had not been brought up frum). She had married a chain-smoking, blue-eyed man she met through a matchmaker. Tova was enjoying a brief time of freedom before the first of what would surely be many pregnancies.

Kingston Avenue had many amusements to keep me occupied.

There were the "kosher pizza murders." In the back of the restaurant hung a thick red curtain. Every so often I would watch as another long-white-bearded Hasid would open the curtain and go in. I craned my neck to see what was back there, past the piles of boxes, but the curtain always shut before I could see anything. The old men never came out. It didn't matter how many hours we sat; no one came out.

"What, are they killing them back there?" I whispered to the girls.

One day, I couldn't take it anymore and shot past the Israeli pizza man before he had a chance to stop me and thrust myself through the curtain. There, sitting around a large bong, were three pious old men smoking their brains out on what smelled like some really good weed.

"It eez kosher . . . you know," Fagee purred in her rich accent, and we all burst into giggles.

There was also the "Shabbas roller," a Hasid with a spectacularly long black beard that nearly touched his knees. He dealt with the pre-Shabbas rush—trying to get the errands done before the cutoff time when you could no longer spend money, bathe, or do anything work related— by lacing up a pair of roller skates and racing through the neighborhood at full speed. His wondrous beard would trail behind him like black streamers as he raced by. "Woo hooo!" I would yell. He would smile as he whizzed past, shouting, "Good Shabbas!"

Months after moving to the apartment, I was invited to a special event where the rebbe was to give blessings to women. I waited for hours on line, and when my turn came, he pushed forward a small plastic cup of wine. I stared at the cup, not knowing what to do. He nodded his head and motioned toward the wine. Finally a chorus of women yelled, *"Drink it!"* so I did.

Later on, my friends cooed, "Do you realize he was giving everyone else bread and you a cup of wine?"

"He must have taken one look at me and decided I needed a drink!" I answered.

It's an irony to say that the rebbe, who inspired countless thousands to become more religious Jews, is the reason I abandoned my pretense at religious life, but he inspired me to be true to myself. If he saw something special in me, as I was convinced he had the day of the wine, maybe I was fine just the way I was. Bad ass!

It happened quickly. On a Monday, I put away my Salvation Army maxi skirts. By Wednesday, I was wearing tight jeans and safari wear. I loved to wear vintage army uniforms because I really did feel like I was at war.

Sadly, this did dry up the free dinner invitations, but it was a small price to pay for feeling like I was populating my own skin again.

I became a walking message that joy and pride could be felt, even by a woman in pants.

After a phenomenon I would later understand as an illegal eviction, I landed my own place farther down Kingston Avenue. It was a large two-bedroom over the pharmacy, and I decided to share the $250-a-month rent with my overly perfumed French pal, Fagee.

An artist friend of mine gave me an easel, and I scrounged together enough money to buy acrylic paints.

The first painting I did was of Grace Jones. The second was the rebbe. Hey! I was diversifying.

We celebrated our new home by throwing parties for local starving artists and any Jewish outcasts brave enough to attend. I was head cook; Fagee's job was to roll the cigarettes . . . and anything else that could be smoked. My culinary palette included whatever was left of the most recent kosher food my mother had sent. My specialty was stir-fried Hebrew National hot dogs and macaroni with burned ketchup sauce. It was a feast fit for a low-budget queen. I was also famous for tuna fish, ziti, and canned-pea casserole. Both of these tasted fabulous after six beers.

Money was too tight for a phone, so I got my messages through the Puerto Rican deli across the street.

"Mi'ijitaaaa . . . Rossitaaaaa . . . you gottaaa message," Hector would yell from the street. "Thank you, Papi!" I would yell back, to the horror of the Hasids, who didn't see anything remotely tzniut about this arrangement.

One afternoon at the pizza joint, a tall, clean-shaven young man wearing a small yellow yarmulke and oddly matching yellow T-shirt walked up to me. He had a wide, silly smile.

"I'm Mickey, and I've been watching you for a while. You're just what we need around here." Then he let loose a high-pitched girlish laugh that made it impossible to not laugh too.

"Are you Lubavitch?" I asked, noting his lack of Hasidic attire.

"My family is, but I'm . . . something else." Clearly.

Mickey Cohen had grown up religious but had shaved his beard sometime around his nineteenth birthday. He still lived at home, a few blocks from me, but went to Manhattan every day to work as a photographer. Mickey was also blessed with something marvelous: his sister's car. Once away from the prying eyes of Crown Heights, all hell broke loose.

One day, a letter came in the mail. In it was a check for five hundred bucks sent to some dead guy who used to live in my place and, amazingly, it came with a check-cashing ID!

Five hundred bucks was like a million dollars to me then. I called Mickey, who immediately snatched the envelope from me and ran away. He came back an hour later, honking the horn of his sister's car, with the money in his pocket.

"I'll pick you up at eight!" he yelled, and drove away, leaving a wake of manic, high-pitched giggles.

We went dancing at the Electric Circus. I wore purple zebra-print pants and a Spandex tank top. Mickey wore black jeans, black sneakers, and a black T-shirt. He would have disappeared on the dance floor if it wasn't for his pink face. We danced like stupid kids who didn't know what rhythm was, jumping up and down and banging into each other like grasshoppers. We had a blast.

At 4:00 a.m. we bought hot-from-the-oven bagels from Dizzy's in the meat market, slathered with cream cheese. I tore apart that hot, gooey, wonderful mess like it was my last meal on earth, the sweat from the dance floor still drying on my stomach. We sat outside, smiling at the hard-working hookers and the butchers grabbing their early morning coffee before an eight-hour shift cutting up cattle.

I was slurping root beer through a straw on the hood of Mickey's sister's car in the center of a place from my dreams. Here I was. This was New York City!

I knew right then and there I had to get to Manhattan.

Salvation came in the form of a phone-sales job for the *New York Times*. Phone sales was an excellent career choice for someone who looked like Courtney Love on acid. I had a husky voice and didn't take no for an answer. I did well and put every extra cent aside for my future home in Manhattan. With my savings, and a small inheritance I came into when I turned eighteen, I left Crown Heights and moved into an apartment in the George Washington Hotel on Twenty-Third and Lexington. For $400 a month, I had my own phone, a bed, a set of dresser drawers, a private bath, and twenty-four hours of room service offered by the same diner that had once employed Rita Hayworth.

Late one afternoon, I checked in with two suitcases of new wave clothing and a shopping bag of art supplies. By morning, I had all but forgotten Kingston Avenue. Or so I thought.

"You can leave Kingston Avenue," the kosher-dairy shopkeeper once said to me, "but it's always on you. The road sticks under your feet."

Years later, when I heard the news of the passing of the great rebbe, I looked at the bottoms of my black leather ankle boots and sighed.

## Easiest Jewish Chicken Soup
## This Side of Brooklyn

*Serves up to 10 people*

### INGREDIENTS

*4 (8 oz.) cans kosher chicken broth*
*3 boneless chicken breasts, chopped*
*3 white onions, chopped*
*2 drizzles olive oil*
*1 heaping handful carrots, peeled and diced*
*1 heaping handful celery, diced*
*1 pinch salt, fresh ground pepper, dried dill, paprika,*
   *and garlic powder*
*1 lb. kosher egg noodles*

Bring about 4 cans of kosher chicken broth to a boil.

Drop in your breasts. (No, not your breasts! Your chicken breasts!)

Lower heat to medium and simmer for 20 to 30 minutes. Remove your breasts (your chicken breasts!) from the broth. You can cut open a breast to make sure it's fully cooked. It's okay to cheat.

Chop up about 3 onions and sauté in olive oil till soft and add to your soup.

Then throw a heaping handful of diced carrots and diced celery into the soup.

Cook for about 20 minutes or until the veggies are soft.

Throw your chicken into the soup.

I like to season Jewish style: salt, pepper, dill, paprika, garlic, and guilt, but you can adjust to your liking.

This is freezable, once cooled, and you can serve as is, but to make a real meal out of it, serve with Jewish-style egg noodles. Oy vey!

# Stabbing Magdalena

My mother tried to stab Magdalena with a steak knife. There, I said it.

For years I've wondered if I might have imagined the moment when my mother picked up the knife she'd been using to saw through a not-quite-defrosted Entenmann's coffee cake and attempted to plunge it into the flesh of my good friend and occasional lover Magdalena.

But let me back up, just a little.

I was fifteen when I met Mag. She was twenty-two.

My friend Jen had coerced me into joining a community theater. It was the best favor she could have done me to help me survive an überrepressed, preppy high school in Rumson, New Jersey, where Izod golf shirts and khaki pants were a required uniform. Coming face to face with my first gay, bisexual, and we-don't-give-a-hoot-whom-you-sleep-with friends was a gift from the gods.

I settled in as a back-of-house set person and ersatz mascot. I was an artist, after all. So why not paint sets instead of canvases? The group's ringleader, Matthew (clearly the love child of David Bowie and David Niven), delighted in dragging me to thrift stores and dressing me in vintage prom dresses, then taking me to the Odyssey, the gay disco in Asbury Park. Being allowed into a real disco without being asked for ID, served alcohol, and twirled around on the dance floor by drag queens was the most glamorous thing that had ever happened to me.

It became clear to my parents that someone or something was corrupting me: a change in clothing, a distant attitude, the slipping of grades.

But it was not Matthew my mother hated: No, his charming, well-spoken demeanor gave her calm. But Mag, who stood seven feet tall in heels, who had the shoulders of a linebacker and the face of Bette Midler on steroids, who boldly wore miniskirts that barely covered her derriere, who smoked long cigarettes from plastic holders, and who rarely spoke below a screech—this woman made my mother very uncomfortable.

When I started to smoke, drink, stay out late, and carry on with boys and girls in all sorts of wicked ways, my mother didn't blame my party-hearty friends. She was convinced that hell had come spewing forth through the tall woman blowing smoke rings at the picnic table in our backyard. Nothing right could come from someone who looked so wrong.

Magdalena was not my first lover and certainly not my last; to be truthful, even by that tender age of fifteen, she was one of several females who had graced my bed, or rather the backseat of my parents' Volaré, but when Mom got an inkling that her middle child might not exactly be heterosexual, it was Mag she blamed.

"Magdalena! She's ruining my Shana Madelah!"

When I wound up, like it or not, living in Crown Heights, Mom consoled herself: "My beautiful little girl is out on her own too young . . . but at least she is away from Magdalena!"

Little did Mom realize that Mag had been spending weekends with me in my funky bachelorette pad. She'd arrive on a Friday night as the neighborhood was rushing home to prepare for the Sabbath—Magdalena plowing down Kingston Avenue in a fuchsia minidress and red vinyl go-go boots, sending Hasids in black suits scurrying left and right like the parting of the Red Sea.

I loved to hang my head outside my window overlooking Kingston to take in the sight.

"Rossalinda," she would screech from two blocks away, "I'm heeeeerrreee!"

When Mag came to town, it felt like a party. As hundreds of our neighbors scurried to the synagogue to begin Sabbath prayers, I would turn up the volume on my cheap stereo, and we would dance around my apartment singing along to my B-52s album, devouring the kosher salami the Big H, my mom, Harriet, had mailed me in soggy freezer packs with mustard and Tam Tam crackers. We'd wash it down with cheap beer from the bodega across the street.

"Hector!" I would scream to my buddy at the bodega, "Send over another six pack of cervezas!"

Who needs a phone anyway?

As big as Mag was, she considered herself a delicate flower. Once the sun had gone down, she would change into a pink lace nightie with matching panties.

"Ain't I pretty?" she'd screech, twirling in front of the mirror.

In the morning, we would lounge on my milk crate furniture or the one real piece I owned, a couch, and drink Bustelo coffee accompanied by big hunks of Italian bread, a fifty-cent treat in my low-rent life.

It was during our Bustelo and bread siesta one Saturday morning in 1982 that my parents showed up for a surprise visit.

I opened the door after hearing the loud banging and assumed it was one of my ruder pals, only to find my parents and a half-dozen bags of kosher groceries at my door.

"You need to eat more!" my mother said, pushing past me before I had a chance to warn Mag.

I followed my mother up the stairs, making a point to yell, "Well, MOM, so nice to have this surprise visit, MOM!"

I heard a pronounced "EEEK" from the living room as Mag raced to assemble herself.

When my mother reached the top of the stairs and came face to face with Mag, in her pink lace ensemble, complete with bread crumbs in her cleavage, she froze.

"Hello, Mrs. Ross. Nice to see you again," Mag said.

My mother said nothing. She stared Magdelena up and down and got a tired, beaten look on her face, then dragged her grocery bags into the kitchen and dropped them on the counter. Mom stood there for a moment, motionless, and then reached into one of the bags and pulled out a not-quite-unfrozen coffee cake. She found a small steak knife in the dishwashing rack and sat down at the kitchen table and began to saw.

I don't know what she meant to do with the cake. The Big H was diabetic, so it may have been some sort of blunted suicide attempt. In midsaw, my mother held the knife in front of her face, then thrust it into the air in a fury.

An eerie, high-pitched voice came out from between her clenched teeth, "I'll kill you, Magdalena!" Then, to emphasize her intent, she stood up and began to wave the knife back and forth.

By this time, Mag had pulled on her pink leather minidress, go-go boots, and matching leather jacket and shoved her undies and toothbrush into her purse. Taking one look at my mother, she made a break for the stairs.

"Rossalinda . . . your mother seems to have gone nuts . . . Time to go . . . Love you . . . Call me!"

Shuffling as fast as her bulk would allow, my mother hobbled down the stairs after Mag, screaming, "Stay away from my daughter!"

I hung my head out the window. Mag, with her long legs, was already two blocks away, racing past the stunned Hasids, but my mother went after her, huffing and puffing and waving the little steak knife left to right.

"Magdalena! I'll kill you, Magdalena!"

Mom never caught Mag, thank the Lord, but I've always wondered just what she would have done if she had.

I laid down the law when my mom returned—I would be eighteen in six months, nearly legal, and the days of surprise visits were over. Much as I wanted and, okay, needed the free groceries, it was better to starve than to be subjected to this kind of humiliation, not to mention near homicide.

My mother, insulted, red faced, and probably still in shock, left the butchered coffee cake on the table, grabbed my father's arm and left.

My dad managed to squeeze in, "Goodbye!" before following my mother down the stairs.

"Marty! We're not wanted here!" screamed my mother, slamming the door.

I sat down at the dinette and stared at the massacred cake. The marks on it could have been made by a serial killer. Would my mom actually have done it? I picked up a piece of cake and popped it in my mouth. Like most of the frozen cakes Mom brought me, it tasted stale.

As the years went by, the story seemed too absurd to be real. Had my mother really tried to stab Mag? I preferred to pretend that my childhood couldn't have been that warped.

Twenty-five years later, at a reunion of the Barn Theatre, a tall, skinny woman smoking Mores with a long plastic filter came up to me. She was older and underweight, but I recognized her immediately.

"Rossalinda . . . darling," she said, squeezing me in her arms. "Remember when your mother tried to stab me with the steak knife?

# Leftover Entenmann's Cake with Pudding

*Serves up to 6 people*

So what to do with all the cake your mother never ate because she was too busy trying to stab your lover? This dessert is ridiculously sweet and messy and fun, just as life should be!

### INGREDIENTS

*1 leftover Entenmann's cake (coffee cake, lemon cake, pound cake, any white cake)*
*1 prepared package of any kind of pudding (I like banana Jell-O pudding)*
*1 coffee cup heavy cream, whipped*
*1 handful maraschino cherries*
*1 handful chocolate chips*

Slice leftover cake into breadlike slices and lay them in a baking dish.

Make any kind of pudding that helps you bounce back from mom rage—vanilla, chocolate, banana, strawberry, whatever it takes—and chill well.

Whip up some cream; you'll want enough to cover your sliced cake.

Fold about half the whipped cream into the pudding, and spread the mixture over your sliced cake.

Top it with the rest of the whipped cream, and top
that with almost anything—candies, nuts, maraschino
cherries, chocolate chips, bits of stiletto heels left behind
in the escape—and chill.

## Rossi's Super-Tacky Chinese-ish Fruit Cocktail Chicken

*Serves up to 4 people*

This recipe was born when Hector started selling four cans of fruit cocktail for a dollar.

**INGREDIENTS**

**CHICKEN**

*4 boneless chicken breasts*
*1 coffee cup pineapple juice*
*1 shot soy sauce*
*1 drizzle vegetable oil*

**SAUCE**

*1 can fruit cocktail*
*1 shot soy sauce*
*2 packets Chinese restaurant mustard*

Cut up chicken into one-inch cubes and marinate in pineapple juice mixed with a shot of soy sauce and a drizzle of vegetable oil anywhere from two hours to overnight.

Bake at 400 degrees for about 20 minutes or until it's cooked through and started to brown.

Meanwhile, mix a can of fruit cocktail with a good shot of soy sauce and 2 packets of leftover Chinese mustard. Bring to a boil and cook until the sauce starts to thicken. When your chicken is done, pour over with your hot cocktail sauce and enjoy!

# The Matthew Rousseau

Leaving home clearly had not turned out to be as glamorous as I'd hoped. Selling the *New York Times* got harder and harder the more bored I got. Still, the *Times* was one of the few establishments that would hire a girl with a safety pin dangling from her ear. I did my best to keep things interesting, perfecting a newspaper subscription pitch that sounded like phone sex: "Mr. Smith . . . I promise you will get it every morning!" I'd say in a raspy Mae West voice. But even this dulled after a year and a half and three-thousand-plus hang-ups triggering my fear of rejection. I resigned and took a job selling wholesale cosmetics at an outdoor market in Soho, a job that lost its appeal in the winter as my own lips turned blue while selling frozen Frosted Rose lipstick to tourists.

One night, while warming myself at a local watering hole, I watched a bartender stir up a perfect martini . . . in a heated room. An alarm went off in my brain. At the grand age of nineteen, I decided to become a bartender.

I had some money saved from frozen-lipstick sales,

so in the winter of 1983 I enrolled in bartending school. The school had enticed me by boasting about the glamorous, big-money bartending jobs students landed via its job-placement service for those talented enough to graduate from this illustrious two-week course.

The only job the service sent me out for was a stint tending bar at the Lismar Lounge in the East Village, where the clientele was far more interested in shooting up in the bathroom than having a perfectly stirred, not shaken martini. I lasted two days.

I let the school send me out for private home bartending jobs to help pay the rent while I searched for a steady gig.

Most of the Help Wanted ads in the *Village Voice* that would even consider a woman as bartender also read, "Must wear leotard!" Keep in mind that this was the eighties, and women tending bar were only sought after by truck stops and strip clubs.

I decided to apply for the one job that let me work in an outfit that wasn't transparent, a day shift bartending on a boat.

It took a lot of courage to walk aboard the *Matthew Rousseau* that afternoon in 1984, and not just because I was a female bartender. Since the day I nearly threw up from watching other kids on a seesaw, I've known that I have more than a small motion-sickness problem. In fact, I have Godzilla-size equilibrium issues.

The lady in the ticket booth at South Street Seaport told me I could go aboard during the twenty-minute gap between cruises. I'd popped a Dramamine and raced down the gangway and onto the deck in search of some guy named Rick. A toothless man with a Cockney accent directed me: "Pasty bloke; you'll find 'im on the upper deck!"

I walked to . . . the bow? Never did get the hang of boat lingo . . . and climbed the back stairs. A rather frightened-looking man with thick glasses was walking along the top deck, talking to himself.

"Are you Rick?"

"When I have to be."

"I'm here for the bartending job."

He sized me up, a smile creeping across his face.

"We're about to leave on an hour-and-a-half cruise up and down the East River. Stay for the cruise, check out the bar action, and we'll talk when we dock back at the seaport."

With that, he spun around and walked away.

I popped another Dramamine.

The *Matthew Rousseau* was a replica of a large Mississippi riverboat. The tub ran short cruises up and down the East River for tourists during the day and rock 'n' roll cruises for aging yuppies at night. The interior of the boat was more 1980 than 1880. There were far too many plastic chairs around plastic tables to maintain any illusion of the Old South, and the Coney Island–style hot dog stand placed it firmly in Yankee territory.

I climbed the back stairs to the top deck, where the open air and surprisingly majestic scenery took my breath away. We floated past what looked like a haunted castle shrouded in weeds. Someone said it was the sanitarium that had housed Typhoid Mary. I'd never seen the old castle and hadn't even known Roosevelt Island existed.

The slow, even ride felt more like being on a train than a boat, thank God. Even *I* could have skipped the pills. Unfortunately, I'd already taken them. After the second one took hold, I was so stoned I could barely keep my eyes open. When the Statue of Liberty came into view, I swear she waved.

I tottered downstairs and watched two harried women try to keep up with the long line at the bar. It was easy to tell the passengers were out-of-towners; no one else wore those "I (Heart) New York" T-shirts.

The bar was well stocked with liquor, but the "I (Heart) New Yorkers" wanted beer, soda, and chips. Giant oil cans of Foster's Lager were the biggest sellers, maybe because normal drinkers could finish just one on a ninety-minute cruise. Had there been any "normal drinkers" on board, that is. This crowd was ready to party and came back for seconds.

The head bartender had reddish-brown hair, flushed ivory skin, and a heavy Irish accent.

"Come on man . . . where's my ice!" she bellowed at a teenage boy. Her name was Elaine. A younger woman, Erin, could have been Elaine's pretty younger sister. She didn't have an accent but looked just as Irish.

The line that owned the *Matthew Rousseau* liked men at the helm, men managing the boat, and men as deckhands, but they were partial to women behind the bar.

"They like to see ladies suffer," Elaine told me. "Most men do."

The captain also liked to see the passengers suffer. The cruise complete, the boat docked with a resounding thud, part of Captain Dave's sense of humor.

"He likes to scare the tourists," Rick said. I jumped at the sound of his voice, having been caught up in the drama of old ladies screaming as we docked. "It's what gets him up in the morning."

I watched as the red-faced beer drinkers, the old ladies, the giddy children, and the Japanese tourists piled down the gangway. A line for the next cruise was already forming and had snaked its way down the pier to the ticket booth.

"I hate summer," Rick said.

"So, um, about the job—"

"Do you have experience?"

"Yes, and I graduated from the International School of Bartending. I—"

"I never met a bartender who went to bartending school."

"I know. I get that all the time—"

"Come back tomorrow at nine," he said.

"Tomorrow?"

"You'll need khaki pants. We'll give you the *Matthew Rousseau* shirt."

"So, I got the job?"

"The better question is, will you want the job?"

My first day on board the *Rousseau*, I served up more Cape Cod–style potato chips than anything else.

"Why Cape Cod chips?" I asked Adeen.

"Oh, the Pencil loves those salty bits of rubbish."

"The Pencil?"

The Pencil turned out to be Seymour, president of East River Lines, a dry, humorless man with an abundance of warty growths on his face. With little on top and perpetually pink skin, he looked like a pencil eraser as he came aboard, hence the nickname.

In the Pencil's mind, the *Matthew Rousseau* docked in Hyannis, not Manhattan.

So we poured Cape Codders (vodka and cranberry) and sold great quantities of Cape Cod chips. Were it not for the expense, we surely would have shucked Wellfleet oysters.

I was branded the outsider at first, partly because I was new, partly because I wasn't Irish, but mostly because I didn't drink beer. Beer, or better yet, Guinness, was an essential part of socializing with those whom I would later call "the boat people."

Over time, I came to understand the world of difference between land folk and boat people.

For one, boat people stuck together. As the thousands and thousands of tourists dwindled each night, boat people would crawl from their galleys, wheel towers, and top decks and meet at either Macduffy's or Carmine's.

Macduffy's was a little bar tucked inside what felt like a secret alleyway in the old part of South Street Seaport.

Boat people deemed the new part, the Pier 17 shopping mall, an abomination. That is until one of the deckhands got a job pouring dark and tans on its top floor. Once his manager was off duty, the mall was considered an abomination with good, free drafts.

Carmine's, a turn-of-the-century Italian restaurant and bar, had weathered the mallification of the Seaport and later endured the booting of the South Street fishing market to the Bronx. This delicious dive had a secret I learned only by hanging with the boat people: Its wildest happy hour was from five to seven. In the morning.

At first I didn't believe it when Ian, Elaine's beau at the time, said he had the hottest shift in the seaport, stepping in when the night boys went home at 4:00 a.m. But as it turned out, the rough-and-tumble men who made their living selling fish in the early morning ended their workday right about then, and they were ready to party.

It's an odd sensation to get off work at two in the morning and walk through the empty seaport, which reeked of old fish, to join a loud and motley crew at Macduffy's, then join a virtual parade to the 5:00 a.m. drinking frenzy at Carmine's.

I stood out, and not just because I was the only person ordering white wine. I was, to my knowledge, the only Jew in the crowd and the only gay person, or at least the only one who acknowledged it. Elaine had taken me under her wing, and when I came out to her, she had an unusual response.

"Oh how delightful!" she screamed. "Fiona!" she yelled

to her cousin at the other end of the bar. "Young Rossi here likes the ladies!"

"How lovely!" Fiona screamed back. Word got around.

"Hey, crazy lady . . . anytime you want a lady, come by my cabin. I got one ready for ya!" Captain Dave said, stepping up to the bar for his fill-up of Jack and Coke.

Captain Dave was beloved by the boat people. He'd fallen for a stripper who looked like Jayne Mansfield and hid her in his cabin for a week. She'd delighted all the deckhands with her occasional drunken live performances.

Dave worked two weeks on and two weeks off, during which time Captain Victor would step in, and we'd all wish we had life insurance. Captain Victor had already grounded the boat once. He only drank wine coolers but couldn't hold those, possibly because he weighed all of one hundred pounds. Where Dave was a rough but jolly sort who loved to socialize, Victor kept to himself. He didn't much care what anyone thought of him.

Boat life as I knew it changed the day I showed up for work and saw a larger, showier riverboat replica docked next to the somewhat bedraggled *Rousseau*. They christened our sister ship the *Edward Brooke*.

She was taller than the *Rousseau* and bore a cadre of just-out-of-college, pretending-to-be-important junior managers. The *Brooke* offered weekend jazz cruises and private parties that finally drew the upper-crust

New England–style crowd to which Seymour aspired. I bartended on both boats and had to admit the *Brooke* was more swank, but a part of my heart felt bad for the upstaged *Rousseau*. I always loved an underdog.

Brian McCallister, of those McCallister tugboats you see putting around with big *M*s on the side, was a big-time investor in East River Lines. We knew this because every time he came on board, the large-and-in-charge junior manager of the moment would run up to us screaming, "Brian is coming!" as if it were Jesus himself.

One of the barbacks was Brian McCallister's son, a good-looking young man just out of high school, who clung to the lowest rung on the boat-people employment ladder. We taunted him endlessly about his dad, but the truth was, we were impressed to see a McCallister hauling trash.

One of my favorite things about tending bar on the boats was Erin. She was my partner, the yin to my yang, the Cher to my Sonny. Erin had an innocent, "good girl" look but was just as gutter mouthed as the deckhands when she wanted to be.

As each rock 'n' roll cruise began, Erin and I would turn to face a line of three hundred yuppies. By the time we got to the end of that line, the cruise was over and another three hundred yuppies were waiting at the dock. You had to keep a sense of humor, or drink. We did a bit of both.

It was the summer of peach schnapps, and no one could get enough of it. Fuzzy navels, sex on the beach, woo woos—it was ridiculous. I never got used to the sight of a three-hundred-pound man saying, "I'd like a woo woo, please."

We got so fast during those cruises that I'd toss her the vodka as her customer ordered a screwdriver. She'd pour peach schnapps into my cup as a secretary in front of me asked for a fuzzy navel. We were one body with four hands.

And we mixed sarcasm with each drink we poured.

"The bloke would like a woo woo," she'd say in a bad British accent.

"Shall we tickle him, then?" I'd ask.

"Nah. 'E'd like that, he would, make him all peachy."

You'd think we would make a fortune, pouring drinks for nine hundred customers a night, but the tourists and the Wall Streeters were cheap. They only left their change. If drinks cost $2.75, they'd leave the quarter. Life got a whole lot better when the East River Lines raised drink prices to $3.25. Erin and I still managed to make $200, sometimes $300 a night . . . in quarters. Same job on dry land would have landed us well in the green.

I started to prefer shifts on the *Brooke* to those on the *Rousseau* because it was newer and the bathrooms were nicer, plus I liked the jazz. My favorite night was when I followed Tito Puente, who said, "Got to get fish for my wife." I'd been pouring him Rémy and Cokes all night long, just to say I hung with the great Tito Puente, but in the early morning darkness, Tito was just a chubby guy trying to keep his wife happy. I liked that.

Then they brought in the Turtle.

Seems that among our ragtag crew, too many Foster's oil cans had gone missing, and a drunken fight or two too many had made the Pencil think we needed the big guns. It also might have had something to do with the investors complaining they saw ladies' underwear hanging to dry on the top deck of the *Rousseau*.

The big guns sent a short, fat, bearded man who looked like a nerdy turtle.

The Turtle introduced an antitheft system. After every shift, our cups were counted. If the money in the register didn't match the number of missing cups, the difference came out of our pay. A kid asking for a cup of water might cost us five bucks.

The Turtle also added nachos with gooey cheese to the bar menu, which we were told to hawk for three bucks a bowl. The cheese always smelled like melted plastic, and it never, ever seemed to wipe off the bar.

The Turtle had a penchant for flight attendants and brought in three to work the bar with us. Erin jumped ship when they added the nacho dispenser and started cup counting; Elaine went ashore to work as a lawyer. Yeah, that freaked me out, too. The Irish babe who'd been opening Foster's alongside me for the last three years was an attorney.

This left me alone with the flight attendants, who, with their frosted hair, foundation, perfume, push-up bras, and gold hoop earrings, made me feel like, well, a guy.

"Hon . . . would you pick that up for me?" they'd ask. "My nail polish is still wet."

The flight attendants didn't last. Neither did the Turtle.

I'd like to say that improved things, but the higher ups had managed to keep the large-and-in-charge junior managers, who were really the worst part. They did ditch the nachos, but nothing short of a *Titanic*-style soak would have removed the plastic-cheese stench.

I spent my last year with East River Lines bartending on the top deck. With the crisp breeze and the gorgeous lights whizzing by, I didn't let the little things get me down. The little things being a major testosteronization of the bar. Seems whoever took over the helm from the Pencil wasn't so fond of women on boats. But it didn't matter anymore. After five years of working side by side with the boat people, I wasn't the same girl who had walked on the *Rousseau*. I looked at the suits and the tourists and the landlubbers and felt pity for them, with a drizzle of contempt.

"Poor bastards," Captain Dave would say, watching the polka-dot neckties march off the gangway.

"Yeah," I'd join in, "poor friggin' bastards."

The day they gave the new boys my best shifts and sent me back to doling out chips and sodas to the daytime crowd, I knew I was done. Not a nice way to repay years of near servitude from a head bartender, which I'd been since Elaine left.

That year, they gave us East River Lines T-shirts instead of Christmas bonuses.

Late at night, Elaine would buy Erin and me rounds at Macduffy's with her lawyer paycheck. Erin had married

Joe, who liked his women not to work; she was only too happy to oblige.

Everything had changed, but I didn't let it get to me that last fall in the seaport. I knew I had one thing that no one could ever take from me.

After five years on the East River Lines, I'd become a boat person, even if I still got sick on swings.

It was in my soul like the scent of nacho cheese. I was, I am, a boat person. And if you don't believe me, you can shove that peach schnapps up your woo woo.

# Cheap and Easy Nachos

*Serves up to 6 people*

The next time you're craving authentic Old South, Cape Cod Mexican, try this.

### INGREDIENTS
*1 (16 oz.) bag corn tortilla chips*
*1 (8 oz.) can black beans*
*A few heaping handfuls grated Monterey Jack*
*    and / or cheddar cheese*

### OPTIONAL
*Pickled jalapeños, sliced*
*Grilled tuna, diced*
*Sour cream*

Fill a baking dish with corn tortilla chips, then open up a can of black beans (I like Goya), drain the water, and sprinkle the beans around the chips. Take a few heaping handfuls of shredded Monterey Jack, and/or cheddar cheese, and pile on top. Use enough to cover your chips, or the cleavage of an average-size flight attendant in a push-up bra, super generously.

Shove the whole shebang into the oven at maybe 350 until the cheese is melted, or better yet put it under the broiler and let that cheese get a nice brown on it!

Then pull from the oven and drop a heaping plop of Sexy

Barmaid Salsa on one side of the nachos and Riverboat Guacamole and sour cream on the other, and let your guests get their hands dirty mishing things up.

I love to put a slice of pickled jalapeño pepper on each chip after it gets cheesed and before it's baked.

For Tito Puente's wife, make grilled tuna nachos by adding diced grilled tuna.

# Riverboat Guacamole

*Serves 2 to 10 people as a topping or one person (me)*
*with a spoon*

**INGREDIENTS**
*4 avocados*
*1 onion, chopped*
*1 plop jalapeño, minced*
*1 plop garlic, minced*
*2 shots fresh lime juice*
*1 handful fresh cilantro, chopped*
*1 pinch salt*

**OPTIONAL**
*1 pinch ground cumin*

Mash 4 ripe avocados with the finely chopped onion, minced jalapeño, minced garlic, fresh lime juice, chopped fresh cilantro, and a pinch of salt.

Mix super well, or do as I do and run the whole mess through the food processor for a second or two.

I like to season this with cumin, too.

## Sexy Barmaid Salsa

*Serves 4 to 6 sexy, sexy people*

**INGREDIENTS**
*10 plum tomatoes, chopped*
*1 onion, chopped*
*1 handful cilantro, chopped*
*1 plop jalapeño, minced*
*Salt*
*3 drizzles fresh lime juice*

Mix about 10 chopped plum tomatoes with one large chopped onion, a handful of chopped cilantro, and minced jalapeño to taste—one jalapeño if you're brave or a half if you're wimpy. Salt to taste and add a few good drizzles of fresh lime juice.

# Birth of a Chef

Tending bar on land wasn't the glamorous life, either. On the boats, it was all about opening cans of lager for tourists and yuppies. On dry land, I mixed martinis for over-the-hill prostitutes with no front teeth.

I was painting my heart out though. Maybe all the work angst fueled my art.

After a dump I bartended at on Seventy-Third and York called Humpty's went out of business (the owners stopped paying the bills, and all the king's horses and all the king's men couldn't get Humpty's out of an eviction again), my roommate Michael, a hardcore alcoholic, landed me a job at a bar and grill in the Flatiron area called Trivia.

Trivia's owner, a middle-aged, gay British man named Roger with a pencil-thin mustache that made him look just like John Waters, preferred to leave the running of the bar to the bartenders. Trivia was a tax write-off for his highly profitable restaurant. My first week there, he gave me a set of keys and said, "Don't steal . . . too much, dear."

Nobody wanted the five-to-midnight shifts Monday through Thursday. Trivia was only busy during weekday lunches when Mark, an adorable, young Brit with a dazzling sense of humor, held court at the bar, and weekends when loads of tourists who didn't know any better wandered in. The weekday evenings were reserved pretty much for Michael, a handful of regulars, and a few people who had been clubbing on Twenty-First Street and needed a place to use the bathroom, do a line of coke, or both.

The food was pretty lousy at Trivia, unless you think frozen mozzarella sticks, frozen chicken wings, frozen burgers, and nachos are anything to rave about, but the drinks were strong, and Mark set the pace by buying back the third round for all the regulars. The tips were decent. Plus, there was the entertainment. Every hour the bartender would scream a trivia question out to the crowd, and anyone who knew the answer would get a free drink. I upped the ante by climbing on top of the bar to scream out my questions.

The Trivia grill cook picked up his shift drink and left around 10:00 p.m., taking with him any patrons who might actually have gone there looking for food, so I had nothing but drunks to look at for the last two hours of my shift. Trying to hold a conversation with people too miserable to stand life sober was getting depressing, not to mention boring.

I started going into the kitchen and digging through the leftovers and creating hors d'oeuvres. I wanted to feed the drunks enough to sober them up so we could hold a conversation and they wouldn't throw up in the bathroom. Picking through the leftovers in the walk-in, I collected nacho chips and cheese and an array of toppings. Stir-fried vegetables, buffalo wings, blue cheese—whatever I could find in the fridge became the nacho of the night.

The strange thing was, that singing-buzzing feeling I got in my chest whenever I finished a great painting also vibrated when I finished making a killer plate of food.

The regulars loved my creations, and I was having far more fun making hors d'oeuvres than I was bartending. Sometimes my creations got a little out there, like when I tried to put hard-boiled eggs and mustard on the nachos, but nobody complained. After all, the main ingredient was sublime: it was FREE!

It was on the *Matthew Rousseau* that I started meeting folks in the catering industry. Sometimes a private party would book the boat, and they'd hire out from a local staffing company for waiters. We'd still bartend, but it didn't take me long to figure out the cater waiters were making fifteen to seventeen bucks an hour to pass out hors d'oeuvres, while we were busting our butts to make ten. I often stuck my nose in the kitchen to watch our perpetually fed-up cook pull roast beefs out of the oven.

"How do you know when they're done?" I'd ask.

"Fuck off!" I quickly learned the language of professional cooks. It was much like the language of our ship's captain and first mate.

"Fuck off, to you, too, but then how do you know when they're done?"

"Stick the thermometer in, and kiss my ass!"

"Got it!'

During one of the private parties, I met a catering captain (sort of like a maître d' or head waiter) named Jake. Jake was super savvy about all the best ways to make an extra buck, so we called him Jake the Snake. He took me under his wing or, um, scale and taught me the basics of cater waitering. I took to waiting tables like a cat to water. I just don't have a submissive bone in my body. I kept getting offended when they'd ask me to clean up their dirty plates.

Jake noticed my knack for cooking and my kooky, creative streak. He started to hook me up with odd catering opportunities, like the guys in Brooklyn who wanted a pro-wrestling cold-cut party. I made a mountain out of salami and other cold cuts and topped it with pro-wrestling figurines. Seeing that giant sculpture of food jazzed me so much, I felt like Leonardo da Vinci. It was time for me to really learn how to cook.

As a bartender, I pretty much spent my whole first year trying to unlearn everything that school had taught me. Nobody, for instance, really accepts an ounce-and-a-half pour: "Could you put some booze in this glass?" If I was gonna learn how to be a chef, I was gonna do it on the job, not in school.

In the eighties, chefs were hardcore. They drank, smoked, snorted coke, and grabbed hot pans with their bare hands. They weren't the squeaky-clean celebrity chefs you see on the Food Network. Most of the chefs I worked with in these kitchens couldn't say a complete sentence without dropping the F-bomb. Hard rock was the music of choice in these kitchens. Anything else was an abomination. Times have changed, but personally, I still think cooking at any kind of speed should be done to the backbeat of Led Zeppelin, Patti Smith, or the Clash. Exception to this rule: Johnny Cash, of course.

During one of my failed attempts to be a waiter, I met up with a super nasty chef at Avery Fisher Hall. Let's call him Jim. Jim was part of that old school of chefs who hated the front of the house. I'd made the mistake of asking him the ingredients of a dip he'd made. He literally turned purple.

There was only one thing Jim hated more than waiters, and that was a woman in the kitchen. In 1987 my decision to become a chef was not met with enormous waves of enthusiasm in any kitchen, but Jim worked for a big company, a big company that didn't want a lawsuit. So it said yes to my job application, which was probably stamped "TOKEN." The best Jim could do was to try to make me quit. I'm pretty sure he bet his sous-chefs that I wouldn't last a day.

I showed up for work at Avery Fisher Hall ready to be taken seriously. I went out and bought the biggest, toughest pair of construction boots I could find. Sadly, when I was offered a chef uniform two sizes too big, the look I'd imagined as ultra cool turned out to be uber clown. Jim led me down a long hallway past cooking equipment bigger than my apartment. At the end of the hallway was a table up against a wall, on which sat a mountain of strawberry crates. My job was to dip three thousand strawberries in chocolate. I could hear the line cooks laughing at me. I knew they were poking fun because every so often the giggling Spanish would be interjected with *la rubia* (the blond). I don't recall anyone checking to see if I wanted a lunch break, a glass of water, a bathroom break, or any such thing, but I do recall going into some sort of hypnotic zone as I dipped each strawberry in hot, melted chocolate, laid it on a sheet pan covered in parchment paper, and went to the next. I realized I was making seventeen bucks an hour not to be a prep cook but to be a factory worker.

My whole life flashed before me while dipping strawberries in that corner: the bullies I'd endured in grammar school, the oppressive parents I ran away from, the hypocrisy of the Hasids who had shunned me. I was twenty-three years old and felt like I'd been at war for five decades. There was no way I was gonna let smug-faced, red-nosed Jim beat me. As everyone went home, I dipped my last strawberry and went to find Jim.

He was in his office drinking Jack Daniel's.

"You still here?" he asked, shocked. "I thought you left hours ago!"

I took off my apron and threw it at him.

"Listen, you cocksucking bastard: I finished your last fucking strawberry. Now why don't you take them all and shove them up your ass!"

I turned around and started to walk away.

"Wait!" Jim yelled, then smiled wide. "Be back tomorrow morning. I got a big dinner I need help on."

From that point on, Jim called me in as a ringer. He put his regular cooks on the smaller jobs and put me on the big ones. I would still be given not-so-glorious jobs, like making three thousand shish kebabs, but I would also be given an assistant, a lunch break, a coffee break, a pat on the back, and a cocktail or three after work. After a few months, I was promoted and allowed to make salad dressings, dips, and sauces and even go to the party itself and plate food.

It was at one of these events that I met Gérard. Think Gerard, but said in a French accent with the *G* way overpronounced and a bit of spit on the final *D*. It took a lot of practice. Jim was the head chef at Avery Fisher Hall, and Gérard was head chef for all of its New York City holding-company properties, which included the Metropolitan Opera, the United Nations, the US Open, and lord knows what else. But his main mission was to make sure that everyone understood that French people were better than American people, and, more importantly, a French chef would always be far superior to any American chef.

Jim was a rough-and-tumble, all-American cowboy sort of guy, and once I broke him in, we became good buddies. But Gérard never recuperated from the horror of seeing a woman in the kitchen. Bad enough to have to work with Americans, but women? Sacre bleuuuuuu! I soon discovered that Gérard also had a strong dislike for minorities as well, including Jews. So as a full-fledged

American Jewish woman in the kitchen, I was batting a thousand. I didn't bother to tell him I was gay.

We were doing a party for racial equality, with David Dinkins as one of the guests. Gérard had planned the menu, and it was pretty shocking—fried chicken, mini ribs . . . not that these aren't great things to eat, but honey, this menu was two steps from serving pigs' feet.

I was embarrassed about serving this menu to New York's black elite and had taken time to do beautiful decorations on the passing trays with flowers and vines. Gérard walked over to my worktable, grabbed the garnish off the trays, and threw them into the trash.

"Zey are only black anyway!" he screamed. I looked at the smug-faced weasel of a man happily tapping his cigarette ashes over my crumbled flowers in the trash can.

Gérard smoked like a fiend. We all did back then. We kept a glass with an inch or two of water in it to douse our cigarettes.

"Go get me a gin and tonic!" he demanded. In the heat of an event, he liked to demand I fetch him a coffee or a cocktail. You know, just to prove I was a lowly female.

On my way to the bar, I grabbed the cigarette-butt glass and had the bartender fill it with gin and tonic. Gérard grabbed the glass from my hand and slugged down half of it before erupting into hacking fits.

*"Qu'est-ce que c'est?"*

I screamed at him in my attempt at a French accent, "You are only French anyway!"

Then I stormed off, thus ending my career at Avery.

I missed Jim, but I gotta say, to this day, not a moment do I regret one little bit. It had a certain "je ne sais quoi."

I don't really know what happened to Gggggérardddd, but if there is karma, he was demoted and given a female boss, who was, preferably, black, Jewish, and a nonsmoker.

One thing I have to admit about my days at Avery: after making three thousand of anything, you really do get pretty darn good at it. I was a crab cake, shish kebab, chocolate strawberry, and veggie nori roll demon, which really helped in my early catering years. But the first thing I did the moment I opened my own company was to promptly never do any of those things again.

Success is being able to say, *You* make the crab cakes!

Jim ultimately didn't fit in with management at Avery either. They were a sea of yellow neckties with black polka dots, and he was a cowboy who hadn't washed his hair since 1972. He wound up working in a tourist restaurant in Bucks County, Pennsylvania, where all the waiters wore colonial-era garb. I went to visit him once, but it broke my heart. Guys like Jim would be happier in prison kitchens than theme restaurants.

A couple of years after I quit Avery, I became a head chef, and I used the lessons I'd learned working for the big boys.

Rule number one: be nice to the front of the house. If Jim only knew what the waiters he mistreated did to his food, he would have dropped dead. I fed my staff, paid them well, and never yelled at them. They, in turn, smiled at the guests and didn't spit in the food.

Rule number two: never try to cook what you hate. The moment someone calls asking for chicken cordon bleu, I just hang up. A Creole, white trash, Jamaican, Jewish dinner party? That's something I can roll with, Jambalaya, bacon and peanut butter sandwiches, jerk chicken, and latkes.

Rule number three: have fun. Kitchen life can be excruciating—twelve hours on your feet, sweating and cooking. A smile and any opportunity to show just how many food items really do look like genitalia can really make the day flow a little easier. I mean, have you ever taken a good look at a papaya? Downright pornographic!

## Dip-Your-Own Strawberries

*Serves 5 to 20 people depending on how many strawberries they eat*

To hell with dipping three thousand berries. I used to set up a double boiler to melt chocolate for this dish, but then one of my chefs showed me such a simple way to do it I never used a double boiler again!

**INGREDIENTS**
*1 coffee cup heavy cream*
*2 handfuls dark chocolate chips*
*1 shot rum, amaretto, or whiskey*
*20 strawberries*

Just bring a coffee cup of heavy cream to a boil and pour it over two handfuls of dark chocolate chips in a metal bowl. Stir until the chocolate is melted, and you're done! I like to add a shot of booze 'cause I'm that kinda girl. Rum, amaretto, and whiskey are all great!

Arrange your strawberries around a bowl filled with warm chocolate, and let your guests go to town! And they say revenge is best served cold.

## *You* Make the Crab Cakes!

*Serves a little party of up to 12 guests*

**INGREDIENTS**
*1 lb. lump crabmeat*
*1 coffee cup bell pepper, finely diced*
*2 plops jalapeño, diced*
*1 handful cilantro, chopped*
*½ red onion, diced*
*The juice of one fresh lemon*
*Salt and fresh ground pepper*
*2 eggs, beaten*
*1 heaping pinch Cajun spice, ground cumin, and*
*    ground coriander*
*2 heaping plops mayonnaise*
*1 coffee cup bread crumbs*
*Vegetable oil or butter*

Sift through crabmeat and take out any bone or hard stuff, then shred with your fingers.

Add one finely diced bell pepper, any color will do; finely diced jalapeño; cleaned and chopped cilantro; finely diced red onion; the juice of one lemon; salt and pepper to taste; 2 beaten eggs; a good pinch each of Cajun spice, cumin, and coriander; and 2 heaping plops of mayonnaise.

Mix the whole mess up, and if it's dry, add more mayonnaise. Form into little two-bite patties, then roll in bread crumbs. We make these well in advance and put them in the freezer. You can either panfry them to order, or do as we do: just lay them in a baking pan, spread melted butter on top, then bake for 7 to 10 minutes at 325 degrees.

You might wind up with enough to make 20–25 mini crab cakes from this recipe, but it's a crime to make just a few crab cakes. I can make a citizen's arrest, or you can make them all.

Serve at a fun party, or just pull out as many as you need as you need them. Freezers are a gift from the Almighty!

Serve with Cayenne Remoulade, if desired.

## Cayenne Remoulade

*Serve with* You *Make the Crab Cakes!*

**INGREDIENTS**
*1 coffee cup mayonnaise*
*2 drizzles fresh lemon juice*
*1 spoonful capers*
*1 plop Dijon mustard*
*1 pinch cayenne pepper*
*1 pinch paprika*
*Salt and fresh ground pepper*

Mix one coffee cup of mayo with fresh lemon juice, capers, Dijon mustard, a pinch of cayenne pepper, a pinch of paprika, and salt and pepper to taste.

# Like Butter

During one of my ill-fated attempts to learn the front-of-the-house part of the catering business, I was sent out to be a waiter at a large sit-down dinner at the Museum of Natural History. At a dinner for three to five thousand people (you really lose count after hitting one), I met a sweet little gay boy named Alex Alexander. He had red hair and freckles and a soft voice but could go full-scale fury at the sight of stupidity, or, for that matter, bad hair. Alex was my "A" waiter. I thought I could not feel any smaller shoved into the old tuxedo I'd bought at a vintage clothing store for fifty bucks, but then I looked up at the giant blue whale hanging above me and felt like a goldfish in a school of dolphins. I was the "B" waiter, which meant I was a lower-rung waiter and Alex's assistant. He took me under his wing, partially because he felt sorry for me and mostly because he was certain I would pour hot soup on somebody's lap, possibly on purpose, and he wanted to watch.

A couple weeks later, Alex and I ran into each other in an arena in which I was far more comfortable: Gladiators, the dive gym where I worked out. Gladiators, located on Sixth Street between Avenues A and B, was a blast from the past, even back then. The walls were plastered with seventies bodybuilding posters and photographs of its mostly Hispanic members striking poses, as well as movie posters from *Conan the Barbarian*. I got a kick out of lifting weights in the small, sweaty hole-in-the-wall, but not as big a kick as the motley crew of tough guys got out of seeing a blond woman in cutoffs on the leg press.

It was in this environment that I met Alex by chance. A few dirty jokes later, in between bench presses, we were fast friends.

Alex was the catering manager for Cynthia Catering. Sounds big, but this was a two-person company run out of Cynthia's apartment. Cynthia was fortyish but dressed like a sixteen-year-old girl, a rather horny sixteen-year-old girl with zero body fat. She had two missions in life: to lower the fat level of everyone she met and to marry a very rich man. She called everyone she met "sweetie," but it came out more like the screech of a high-pitched siren.

When I told Alex I was not really a waiter but a chef (really a chef in training), he got me in as Sally's (Cynthia's chef) number two for a party on a boat. I got so stoned from taking two Dramamine that I threw out some gorgeous watercress leaves and put the stems in the salad. The next week, Sally quit, and with no head-chef experience whatsoever, I got the job.

Cynthia would call me each week with the menu. She was all about New Orleans that year, which may not sound thrilling today, but it was rather avant-garde in the late eighties.

"Sweetie, one hundred people on Friday . . . it's a buffet. I need jambalaya, shrimp Creole, and blackened redfish. Fat-free, of course. Thanks, sweetie!"

With that, I would run out and buy cookbooks with recipes for all the dishes and cook them two to ten times in my apartment for all my guinea pig friends. Once my friends were satisfied that the food was sublime, I would show up to work as an expert. This was years before the Internet, so my apartment was quickly becoming a library of cookbooks, and my friends were stuffed and happy.

I'd never even heard of jambalaya in 1988. The fat-free part, well, I just pretended I didn't hear her most of the time. She had found a product called Butter Buds, a fat-free dry mix that she swore tasted just like butter when you mixed it with water. Nothing mixed with water tastes like butter.

"Use the Butter Buds, sweetie!"

"Yes, Cynthia," I said, knowing I would instead drop a pound of sweet butter into the sauce.

"Are you comfortable with the menu, sweetie?"

"Sure I am, been cooking it for years!"

I made one of the smartest decisions of my life and hired Alex's friend Adam as my sous-chef. Adam had worked at Le Bernardin, and was a well-trained, talented chef with no pretension. He was gorgeous, kind, funny, Jewish, and as gay as the day is long. We fell madly in love. I even thought about having his baby, well, for about two minutes. I had two cats, and that was quite enough commitment for me.

"Adam," I'd say, "make me a beurre blanc." And as he did, I'd watch his every move over his shoulder. Hmmm, so that's how you do it, I thought.

To this day, I credit Adam with having the kindness and egoless dignity to allow me to be his boss and learn from him at the same time. Adam was a lesson in Zen. He never freaked out. No matter how rocky the party was he would just smile and repeat his mantra, "It ain't deep." It almost never was. When I was noting how he made all those mother sauces (the five classic French sauces), he would just smile. I'd like to think I taught him a few things, too, but mostly in the art of having the biggest set of chutzpah imaginable. After all, I did take over a head chef job with about enough cooking experience to work at McDonald's. I lost Adam to AIDS in the early nineties. He died quietly in his family's home in Pittsburg. My handsome superhero could cook a fourteen-hour shift, change into a white leather jacket, and dance the night away, shouting, "It ain't deep! Let's go dancing!"

Then Big S joined our team.

The first time I met Big S, she was stirring tomato sauce, wearing nothing but a black lace bra, matching panties, and an apron. In my kitchen.

All I saw was a six-foot-tall, seminaked woman with a good extra hundred pounds on her.

*Adam at my apartment in the West Village (late eighties).*

"It's hot as hell!" she yelled in an accent that sounded one part western and two parts any big city above the Mason-Dixon line. Oddly, the lady was from San Diego.

Our mutual pal Alex had dragged her in when I complained I was short on prep cooks with a brain. The last couple I'd hired didn't know the difference between chopping an onion and hailing a cab.

I was just about to say something to her about the possible hygiene issues of a seminaked prep cook hovering over a vat of tomato sauce, when she screamed, "Try this!"

I let her shovel a spoonful into my mouth as I finalized the speech in my head: "Now see here, there is no room in a proper kitchen for improper attire."

Then the full and lovely taste of the most gorgeous tomato concasse I'd ever tasted filled my mouth.

The next couple of weeks were a nonstop gastronomic orgasm of delight, with Big S infusing all my New York recipes with a heaping dose of Cali-Mexican and white-trash Southern.

To this day, I add cayenne pepper to my Caesar salad dressing and jalapeños to my apricot jam and proudly think of Big S.

But alas, Big S could only stay in New York for a few weeks at time. She'd come in for the busy Christmas party season and the spring wedding season, then she'd hop back to San Diego in a cloud of hooting, hollering, and fried chicken, leaving me with a craving for cilantro.

I wound up being a chef for Cynthia for three years, and you know what? After three years of looking up recipes and watching my beloved Adam make sauces or Big S show me the true art to slow-cooked meat, I actually did learn to cook.

Two decades later, I ran into Cynthia at a spa in Mexico.

"Did you ever realize that I didn't know what the hell I was doing when you hired me? I had to look up every recipe for everything I made for you!"

Cynthia, by this point, was sixty-something, miraculously claiming to be forty-something, dressed like a sixteen-year-old girl, and still had no visible body fat. She'd been happily living in Boca Raton.

She smiled her ear-to-ear grin and said, "Who cares, sweetie? The food was fabulous!"

Using the safety of a steady check from Cynthia, I started my own fledgling catering company and hired Alex as my front-of-house manager. It was extra money on the side for both of us, and Cynthia didn't mind. I was snagging wacky parties for alternative clients on the Lower East Side or Brooklyn, and she was serving ambassadors and executives. We were hardly competition.

I was developing what would become my forte: outside-the-box weddings.

When eighties excess collapsed into nineties recession, Cynthia's megabudget corporate cocktail parties disintegrated. She closed shop.

"So long, sweetie!" she screamed into the phone, then packed her Butter Buds and her miniskirt collection and flew south. While we were freezing our asses off in New York City, Cynthia was poolside in Boca. Many times it's occurred to me that Cynthia may just have been the smartest person I've known.

Alex started his own catering company and found his niche: gay men so wealthy they didn't notice the economy had tanked. Alex and I kept each other afloat. He would captain my events, and I would be a chef for his.

I thought Alex's food was super fussy and pretentious. He thought my food was too "abundanza," rough and free flowing. In the end, I learned the art of food display from him, and he learned how to make sauces with soul from me. So I'd say we each got the best of the deal.

I lost Alex to AIDS, too. We didn't know about the dementia back then, but thinking back to the day he announced he was quitting catering to become a stand-up comedian, I should have worried. A lot. Alex was many things, but he was not funny. In the last year of his life, he maxed out his credit cards and rehearsed horrific stand-up routines until his friends stopped taking his calls. He ultimately went to a hospital in Virginia where his mom lived and, with his closest friends around him, quietly passed away.

I was by his bedside a few days before he died. He had lost his voice and used a board to write his wishes.

"What can I do for you, Alex?" I asked, hoping for a deep final wish to be scrawled on the blackboard.

"I want strawberry yogurt," he wrote, and smiled.

"You got it," I said, and delivered a strawberry yogurt to the sad, sweet, lonely boy who showed me how to make food look beautiful.

There were down seasons in catering. January and February, you'd be lucky to make a dollar. July and August, you had to go to the Hamptons if you wanted to work.

I didn't mind sleeping off January and February; I was so tired after the Christmas rush that it took two months to catch up. But the summer . . . that's when a girl could really feel a financial pinch.

I went to work on a yacht for a couple of summers. The captain would meet me at the dock, and we'd go to the meat market, to a store called Western Beef, where you could walk inside a giant refrigerated room and buy racks of ribs, filet mignons, gallons of coleslaw, all kinds of huge items at wholesale prices. Most of the shoppers were large Hispanic families buying fifty pounds of chicken wings. This was years before places like Costco existed.

For our "All-American" cruise that would take thirty stockbrokers from New York to Stamford, Connecticut, I bought everything I needed to make barbecued ribs and chicken, potato salad, coleslaw, iceberg lettuce salad, biscuits, and apple pie.

The boat's galley was a tiny, dismal little kitchen, and by the time I had finished the buffet, everything was covered in sauce, oil, and sweat. Then I had to clean up after myself. I'm talking scrub the kitchen down to meet a white-glove test. Literally. The evil twenty-something woman who managed the boat actually came down, put on a white glove, and wiped her finger along my oven.

"Clean it more," she said, and if I could have pushed her overboard from below deck, I might have. Most of the crew felt the same way, but none of us wanted to go to jail.

But the money was sweet. I got paid about 20 percent of the total take—which was often a good grand a day—so, I could suffer a little. I did start to worry that my steady diet of Dramamine, ginger ale, and crackers was going to kill me though, so when I got the boot in favor of a "cheaper" chef, I was happy to go. Besides, I was starting to really miss this thing called land.

# Bring-on-the-Butter Shrimp Creole

*Serves 6 to 10 guests*

## INGREDIENTS

*1 heaping handful each green bell pepper, white onion,
  celery, diced*
*4 heaping plops sweet butter*
*1 heaping plop garlic, minced*
*1 heaping spoonful tomato paste*
*1 coffee cup white wine*
*1 pinch chili powder*
*1 pinch cayenne pepper*
*1 (16 oz.) can tomatoes, any style*
*1 drizzle Worcestershire*
*1 drizzle hot sauce*
*Salt and fresh ground pepper*
*4 handfuls shrimp, peeled and deveined*
*1 good pinch cornstarch*
*1 handful scallions, sliced*
*1 handful parsley, chopped*
*1 lb. white rice, cooked*

## OPTIONAL

*1 coffee cup shrimp stock*

In a deep skillet or pot, sauté a heaping handful each of
diced green peppers, onion, and celery (the foundation
of all great N'awlins cooking) in a boatload of sweet
butter—about 4 heaping plops to be thrown in when

Cynthia isn't looking. After a few minutes, throw in a heaping plop of minced garlic. Sauté until your veggies are soft.

At this point, I like to drop a heaping spoonful of tomato paste in the center of the pan and kind of burn it for a minute. When the tomato paste and my veggies are brown, I toss in a coffee cup of white wine (and drink the rest).

Let that cook for a few minutes until the wine dissolves, then add a pinch of chili powder, a pinch of cayenne pepper, a 16 oz. can of tomato sauce (or whole tomatoes or diced tomato or whatever you have in your cupboard that says tomato on it), a good drizzle of Worcestershire, and Tabasco or some other Louisiana hot sauce if you have it. Add plenty of salt and pepper to taste.

Make sure to pour in all the liquid from the tomato can. Add a coffee cup of shrimp stock, too, if you want to bump this up to killer, but it's way good as is. Bring this baby to a boil and cook for 10 to 15 minutes. Then reduce to a simmer and throw in 4 handfuls of cleaned shrimp. Cook till the shrimp is just done; a few minutes should do it.

A lot of folks like to thicken this up with cornstarch or flour. I'm partial to cornstarch. Just add a shot of water mixed with a pinch of cornstarch in at the boiling stage. But since it's getting poured over white rice, I often leave it nice and saucy.

This gets garnished with a good handful of sliced scallions and chopped parsley, too. But do as you please. It's your shrimp party.

Serve with 4 coffee cups of white rice, cooked however you like it. Since rice can double or triple in size, you're only gonna need two coffee cups of raw rice or about a pound to start.

# Delia's

I'd been a catering cook for three years, taking odd jobs and freelance catering work, but my chef pals told me that I just couldn't call myself anything more than a pot washer until I had some restaurant experience. To call myself a chef, I needed to get my street cred.

I had a friend named Cammy who had an amazing talent for talking her way into well-paying chef jobs. I'd never met anyone who got more plush jobs than Cammy, but she always lost them.

"Cammy, why the hell do they keep firing you?" I asked one day over a bottle of wine, most of which she was drinking. "I don't know," she said in her raspy voice as she lit another Marlboro. "They're just jealous!"

Cammy was hard to forget. She had wiry bleached-blond hair, pale skin always tinged with red, a smile's worth of cigarette-stained teeth, and a screech like a dinosaur coming in for the kill. She was a decade older than me but looked twice my age.

"I got a lot of mileage on these bones!" she said once,

owing to a checkered past that left her with a dragged-around-the-block look.

When I got catering gigs, I would hire Cammy as my number-two chef. When she got catering gigs, she would hire me as her "two," so we kept each other in the money while my business continued to grow. But in the off-season things really dried up. This particular end of winter in early 1991 was unusually bleak. The economy was in the toilet, and so was my mood.

Cammy landed a chef job at a joint I'd never heard of in Alphabet City called Delia's, on East Third Street between Avenues A and B. Back then you never went farther east than Avenue A without looking over your shoulder to see who might be following you.

I did hang out east of A, but in the daytime. My fave cheap breakfast was the Life Cafe's huevos rancheros. Life, a funky dive bar and restaurant on Tenth Street and Avenue B, had become just that—a safe haven for hipsters, artists, and locals of all sorts. The food was cheap and plentiful, and the drinks were strong.

Delia's was owned by a rather rotund woman of the same name, and both the supper club and its hostess had become an underground sensation. I thought Delia was British when I met her. She had a very posh way of speaking. But I was later told she was born in Dublin. It must have been from one upper-crust Irish home because Delia paraded around like royalty.

She wasn't the least bit fazed by American celebrities. Perhaps that's because her long roster of dinner guests included her close friend the exiled princess from Yugoslavia, Princess Elizabeth, Tony Adams, Julie Andrews, Liza Minnelli, and John F. Kennedy Jr.

Nobody back then knew how to entertain like Delia.

The small supper club hosted models, fashion designers, and celebs galore, but its biggest clientele was trust-fund babies. They seemed to delight in the naughtiness of being in the bad part of the East Village and then walking into a high-class lounge. They would line up in their limos and pile in through the velvet ropes as the junkies, punk rockers, and drug dealers looked on in annoyed amusement.

William Kennedy Smith hung out at the bar at Delia's surrounded by pretty preppy girls. Getting charged with rape that year only seemed to enhance his allure.

The reason Delia's supper club felt like Delia's private dining room was because it *was* her private dining room. She greeted all her guests as if they'd come to her home for Irish supper. She lived in an apartment right across the street, and sometimes after-hour guests would wind up there.

Delia's was the first place I ever went to in the East Village that had real candelabras, not to mention antique oil paintings on the walls. She seemed to have a particular passion for horse paintings. Everything was elaborate and weathered at the same time. It was shabby chic before there was such a thing. And I remember burgundy. The first time I met Delia, she was in a burgundy chair, wearing a burgundy frock, and yelling at a waiter. She and the chair had morphed into a large ball of burgundy fury.

Late at night, after the dinner rush, four or five of the center tables would be removed to reveal a dance floor. A DJ would start spinning. I doubt Delia's was large enough to legally entertain the hordes of partiers who lined up to get in—and it certainly lacked a cabaret license—but nobody cared what happened east of Avenue A in those days.

East of Avenue A was a pretty rough scene. There was an out-of-business gas station around the corner that operated as an illegal after-hours club, most buildings were entirely graffiti-ridden, and every fourth bodega was a front for drug dealing. A high-class lounge that let in ten or fifty people too many was the least of the city's problems.

Delia was famous for two things: hosting spectacular parties and shepherd's pie. She would hold court at a table overlooking her fans as if she were the Queen of England. With her platinum-blond hair, she looked like something of an oversize baby doll.

"I'm a former disco queen!" she would often say. It was a bit hard to imagine.

Her husband, Val, a rough and rugged, handle-bar-mustached Russian cab driver, took over as security, guarding the front door and letting in the legion of blue blazers who lined up. The regulars looked like they'd be more at home on the Upper East Side having high tea than twenty feet from a homeless man defecating on the sidewalk.

I'd heard that Val was former KGB, and I didn't doubt it. He was an intimidating ruffian of a guy, but his biggest job was not ejecting drunks but guarding the "secret button." He pressed that button when the police or fire department would come investigating late night noise. The button cut power to the DJ. "What dancing? There's no dancing here. Just a few rich kids pantomiming in the middle of the floor."

Cammy had been working for six months in Delia's kitchen. Since Delia felt anything before 8:00 p.m. was a bore, Delia's did not open its doors before then and stayed open till 4:00 a.m. Owing to the fact that Cammy felt a shift drink was certainly plural, she had been crawling home at five in the morning for so many weeks she forgot what daylight looked like. She decided it was time to train someone to do her job so she could take a few days off now and then, and so she called me.

Aside from landing cushy jobs, Cammy had an enormous talent for creating menus designed to put most of the work on other people's shoulders. When she redid Delia's Irish pub—style menu to be pub meets French bistro, she ingeniously put the hardest jobs on the back of José, the unassuming, young grill man who never could speak back to Delia, Cammy, or probably any strong woman. He had to grill the steak, roast the chicken, sear the fish of the day, fry the French fries for the steak frites, panfry the soft-shell crab, poach the salmon, and cook any meat special.

Cammy's job was to make a cheese plate out of a wedge of Stilton and a wedge of Camembert with grapes and croutons, make the endive salad, sauté the escargot, steam the mussels, and cook the shepherd's pie. Considering that cooking the shepherd's pie meant topping prefilled crocks of cooked-meat filling with mashed potatoes and shoving them under the broiler, Cammy wasn't exactly suffering.

Growing up kosher presented a few chef's challenges for me. To this day, I can't bring myself to eat pork. I was willing to taste shrimp and lobster to understand it so that I could cook it, but nothing, nothing in my Jewish soul would allow me to taste the snails.

On my first and only day of training at Delia's, Cammy showed me how to sauté canned French snails in garlic and butter and add a bit of white wine, then cook just till the sauce reduced and whisk in a thimble of cream.

"Try it!" she screeched. "They're fabulous." I put my finger in the sauce and tasted it for salt. All I could taste, thank god, was cream and butter.

"Sauce is good," I said, refusing to eat what I regarded as a plate of slugs.

Cammy was midway through my first night of training when Delia asked her out to the table to tell her a special request for the night. It had something to do with a table of ten with special dietary restrictions.

"I hate her!" Cammy hollered upon her return. She retreated into a tiny bathroom in the kitchen that had barely enough room in it for a mop and a toilet.

A half hour later, she had not come out.

"You okay in there?" I asked.

"Leave me alone!" she howled.

A table of eight had just been seated, and the head waiter, a fifty-something gentleman clearly upset about still being a waiter, announced in a tone that can only be called terminally bored, "I need two salad, two snail, one cheese plate, and one mussels!"

The entire order was from my station, and Cammy hadn't finished my training. I looked at José, who just shrugged his shoulders and smiled.

Since she hadn't shown me how to cook mussels her way, I did them the way I'd learned. Put a spoonful of minced garlic in a pot and two spoonfuls of butter, put this on high heat and close the pot. Once the butter is melted, drop in a bowl of mussels and a cup of white wine, then cover the pot again. When the mussels opened, they were done.

I started on the mussels and put the snails on to sauté, then spun around and tried to make the salad while worrying about burning the snails. When I turned around, I saw two perfect salads and one cheese plate waiting on the pickup counter. José stood there smiling.

"You are so sweet," I said.

"No problemo," he said in a thick Mexican accent, and I almost kissed him.

An hour went by, with José showing me how to plate

and garnish, and me returning the favor by plating and garnishing his orders, too. Somehow it went okay.

Amid the adrenaline for the dinner rush, I had completely forgotten about Cammy. I looked at the clock and realized an hour and a half had gone by since she'd entered the bathroom.

"Cammy!" I yelled, knocking. There was no reply.

I opened the bathroom door and saw Cammy sitting on the closed toilet. Each of her legs was up on the walls on either side of the door, so she looked spread-eagled. Her head had fallen back against the wall, and she was using the toilet tank as a neck rest. Her arms were wrapped around a three-gallon jug of really, really cheap cooking wine, three quarters empty. She was snoring in little dinosaur squeaks.

I wasn't entirely surprised when two weeks later I got a call from Delia asking if I wanted Cammy's job.

I called Cammy to see if she was okay with it, and she replied, "You can have the stupid job! She's mean and jealous!"

Thankfully, Delia had decided to only open Wednesday through Saturday, so I had three days to recuperate from what turned out to be not such a cushy job after all.

Each day I would come in at ten in the morning to meet José, who thankfully came in at nine so I wouldn't have to. We would begin the prep for the night. I would filet the salmon, prepare the garnishes, and make the dill sauce for the salmon and vinaigrette. José would peel potatoes, scrub mussels, quarter the chicken, and portion the steak.

Then came the only part of the day I looked forward

to: making the shepherd's pie filling. I don't know why I expected Delia's recipe to be something special. When she explained that I should simply "sauté onion and carrot, brown hamburger, season with salt, pepper, and Worcestershire, add peas, and leave it the hell alone!" I was dumbfounded. It was just too simple to be great.

The first time I made it, I did exactly as she asked, and it really was good. But after a few days I grew bored, so I came up with new and intriguing ways to add a smidgen of something that made it taste better but that she couldn't notice. One day, I added a drizzle of A1 Steak Sauce. One day, I added a smidgen of ground coriander. Another day, I added beef stock. The regulars raved about the shepherd's pie, and Delia beamed with pride. "Just like home!" she'd coo, and hand out glasses of champagne.

José and I would prep all day. Then I would make the staff meal at five. No one had told me that staff meals were pasta and bread. I always had trimmings, day-old salad, and leftovers, so I would make mini feasts for the team of six waiters, one bartender, and Val, who was stationed at the door all night long. My first staff meal was Caesar salad, sautéed salmon, asparagus, and parsley mashed potatoes. The staff thought I was a god.

"Waste of bloody fish!" Delia yelled, but quickly demanded Val bring her a double helping.

We would serve dinner till the kitchen closed. Delia let us know if there was a private party the next day, and if there was, we would have to stay on after the dinner shift to prep items for the next day.

"Private party for fifty!" Delia announced one night,

and I was left cursing and teary eyed, filleting salmons, cooking an extra batch of shepherd's filling, and making large cheese platters while José peeled potatoes. It was 2:00 a.m. and we were both miserable. I put all the party food in the walk-in and crawled home to the West Village.

The next day when I came in, I found José scratching his head. In the walk-in, the salmon looked as if it had been clawed by a bear. It was literally hacked apart. The shepherd's filling was nearly gone. A good portion of it was on the floor in the walk-in. The Stilton had bite marks in it.

"What happened?"

"Sometimes after everyone's gone . . . Delia, she gets hungry," José said, patting me on the back. "Mucho hungry."

The salmon was unusable for anything except mousse. There was a sizeable amount of platinum-blond hair in what was left of the shepherd's pie filling. We had to start over.

That night, in the middle of the busiest part of the dinner rush, Delia sent word through a waiter that she demanded supper, a rare steak for her friend and shepherd's pie for herself.

This was one of Delia's favorite nocturnal habits, waiting till the worst part of the night, then demanding her own meal. And it, of course, had to be pristine. It was hard to imagine she was hungry after having hacked through a buffet for fifty.

We'd been so busy catching up on the private party that José had run out of steaks. I pulled out a New York strip still in the plastic from the butcher and cut off a crappy endpiece that was shaped like the state of Florida. José looked at it.

"She's not gonna like this . . . "

I didn't have to ask whether or not I was fired that night; I just collected my stuff.

"I'm gonna miss you, Joselito," I said, and hugged him. It was only then that I noticed that José, who was probably not a day over twenty, had rings around his eyes that could circle Saturn.

The next day Cammy called me, dinosaur-screeching and laughing, "Whadya do? She was so desperate, she even called me. I told her to stick it!"

"Oh honey, she's just mean and jealous!" I said, and we both cracked up.

I heard through the waiter grapevine that José had to jump in and run the line all by himself. He'd been working there for two years, but Delia had refused to believe that a Mexican man had chef potential. When I bumped into the fifty-something waiter on Avenue A, he was beaming with pride.

"The little imp is really knocking it out of the park!" he said.

Evidently, José stuck to my revision of the shepherd's pie recipe, and everyone thought it was the best it had ever been.

I didn't know it yet but the East Village I knew was about to vanish. On Memorial Day weekend in 1988 the police attempted to enforce a park curfew by pushing out the homeless people living in Tompkins Square Park. Tensions erupted, causing what would become known as the Tompkins Square Park Riot. When the dust settled, change had been set into motion. The yuppie-i-zation of the neighborhood was official. "Tent City" in Tompkins Square Park was replaced by baby carriages and dog walkers. Crime got pushed out, and businesses of all kinds, not to mention a boatload of condos, got pulled in.

My beloved Life Cafe became a tourist attraction. A few years later the play *Rent*, written about a group of misfit pals who hung out at the Life Cafe, became a huge hit on Broadway. I'll never forget the first day I trudged across the newly kid-friendly Tompkins Square Park to breakfast at Life and was told there was a half-hour wait for a table.

When I look back on it, I realize that my rough-and-tumble ways dissipated along with the graffiti and the crime of the East Village. With the loss of that gig at Delia's, I began to put serious effort into pushing my fledgling catering business into the stratosphere. My motivation was simple: I was about as employable as I was demure. I needed my own company.

# Not Delia's Shepherd's Pie

*Serves 6 to 8 people, depending on how much meat you put in the ramekins*

**INGREDIENTS**
*1 onion, diced*
*1 drizzle olive oil*
*2 heaping handfuls carrots, peeled and diced*
*2 lbs. ground beef*
*1 shot Worcestershire*
*Salt and fresh ground pepper*
*1 coffee cup beef stock*
*2 lbs. Idaho potatoes, peeled and diced*
*2 heaping plops sweet butter*
*1 coffee cup frozen peas, thawed*
*1 smidgen coriander*

**OPTIONAL**
*Ketchup*
*A1 Steak Sauce*
*Heavy cream*
*1 handful frozen corn, thawed*
*2–3 egg yolks*

Sauté one large white or yellow onion, peeled and diced, in olive oil. Add a heaping handful of peeled and diced carrots. You can either take the veggies out of your pot or use a separate pot, but you now want to brown about 2 lbs. of ground beef. When I say brown, I really do mean cook till brown, then drizzle a good shot of Worcestershire and salt and pepper to taste. Mix in with your sautéed veggies, add a coffee cup of beef stock, and cook another 10 minutes. In the last few minutes, you can add your peas, and if you like, a handful of corn, or a handful of nothing at all.

Now, this is the end of a traditional shepherd's pie recipe. I like to stir in a smidgen of ground coriander and a little drizzle of steak sauce, preferably A1. Sometimes (very often) I add a spoonful of ketchup, but then I am a white-trash gal at heart!

Meanwhile, peel and cut up about 2 lbs. of potatoes, any kind, and boil in salted water till soft. Mash or puree your potatoes, adding a few heaping plops of sweet butter and salt and pepper to taste. This is good to go, but if you're a cream lover, you can add a shot or two of heavy cream. If you like some extra golden glory in your mash, fold in a couple of egg yolks into your mashed potatoes.

I like to use French onion soup—style crocks. Just fill with meat and top with mashed potatoes, then bake at 400 till the potatoes start looking crusty. Or you can put them under a broiler, and things will get really crusty!

I also serve this as an hors d'oeuvre by filling mini tart shells with the meat and piping the mashed potatoes in a pretty swirl on top from a piping bag then heating just till warm.

For a great, easy cocktail party idea, go out and buy Chinese porcelain soup spoons, fill with hot shepherd's pie filling, and top with mashed potatoes then serve as an hors d'oeuvre. Folks go mental for it!

# The Amazon Club

In the summer of 1991 I got a call to cook at a new and unusual New York City supper club called the Amazon Club (known to some as the Amazon Village). I didn't have much else going on and it sounded interesting, so I took it.

The restaurateurs who created the Amazon decided to turn Pier 25 into a mini Brazil. They dumped two tons of sand on the pier, filled it with palm trees, and added outdoor seating. Then they dragged in a few trailers, the kind you see in construction sites. One of those trailers had a pickup window, an oven, a grill, a stovetop, two deep fryers, and a salad counter. That was my kitchen.

Aside from reminding me of Passover, the trailer was perfect for feeding fifty, but for a large-scale supper club? Think psychosis stew.

I had heard that the first chef had a nervous breakdown behind the line. They took him away in an ambulance screaming, "The fish is eighty-sixed! You're eighty-sixed! I'm eighty-sixed!"

Then they brought in Eric, a sweet guy who was more

of a hardcore short-order cook. Eric didn't give a hoot about fresh herbs, but he knew how to get the job done. He hired Sarah, a sous-chef who didn't give him crap, which was pretty much the best a chef could hope for.

He thought he was doing okay. Then the private parties started.

We would receive word from one of the promoters—a trio of hipsters who specialized in attracting the coveted young, chic, and gorgeous crowd. Cornelius was the leader of the trio. He looked a bit like a Vegas lounge lizard with his slicked-back pompadour. Cornelius called everyone, even the dishwashers, "babe."

"Babe . . . just do some barbecue thingy. You know . . . the rib scene. We've got models coming. They don't eat anyway. Got it, babe? Cool."

By the time I got the call, Eric was two steps from locking himself in the walk-in with a bottle of Jack Daniel's and pronouncing himself well done.

I arrived on the faux Tribeca beach at 9:00 a.m. wearing my tough-mama steel-toed boots and a red bandana wrapped around my mass of curly hair. However nervous I was on the inside, I felt my edgy rock 'n' roll chef look would get me through.

As I walked into the trailer, Eric yelled, "Hi Rossi! Nice to meet you. By the way, you're the catering chef, junior sous-chef, and salad babe!"

My section, the cold station, cranked out salads, the cold pasta special, the cold entrée salad special, the celery sticks to accompany the buffalo wings, and a mozzarella and tomato appetizer.

At first I thought I'd be spending my time making pretty salads, but within ten minutes I figured out most of my job would be throwing celery sticks at one of the one-hundred-or-so orders of buffalo wings or throwing tomato and lettuce bundles on one of the two-hundred-or-so burgers a night. When I started to run low on supplies, an old Ecuadoran man with a kindly face would replenish my station. I never had to ask. Eric called him "Grandpa."

As the expediter, Eric started to call out orders as soon as the lunch shift began, "Ordering five burgers medium, four burgers rare, three burgers well, eight wings, two salads, one salmon, one pasta!"

As he shouted, the ticker tape machine would crank out the next order, the one he hadn't read yet. By the time the lunch shift was in full swing, the tape he hadn't read yet was curled out from the machine down onto the floor.

The grill guy, a tall, skinny black man who seemed to be in a constant flurry of motion, preseared one hundred burgers just before lunch and was fresh out within a half hour.

I asked his name.

"Badu," he said.

That quickly morphed into "Bad Dude."

At the end of my first shift, I was covered in salad dressing, salsa, and blue cheese dip. The camper looked like a bomb had gone off inside. The fry guy, whose name was Sammy but who was known as Fry Man, disappeared just after the last calamari was sent out.

"Where's Fry Man?" I asked.

"Gone to reload," Eric said.

"Huh?"

"He's gone to shoot up," Freddy, the sauté man, said. Freddy was the only person working in the kitchen over the age of forty. He was a portly Ecuadoran who ran an Italian restaurant that had closed for the summer. Freddy didn't mind telling everyone he met that he was a real chef and not a line cook. He also didn't mind that nobody cared.

"That was sure a busy first day," I said, feeling proud of myself, then wondering why everybody was laughing.

"This was the lunch shift," Freddy said.

"The dinner shift is the busy one," Bad Dude said.

In kitchens you pretty much always sum up a person by their ethnicity. The Mexican guy, the Ecuadoran lady . . . It's not that cooks are racists—although I'm sure some are. It's just that we don't have the time to delve into proper descriptions. We're in too much of a rush to say, "Yeah, the dark-haired young man with the mustache who speaks Spanish," so it's just, "Yo! Mexican dude, come over here!"

At the Amazon, the night boys were a motley crew of toughies. There was Eric the Red, the nighttime expediter. He wore his long hair in a bun atop his head and worked in a chef jacket he'd cut the sleeves off of. The grill was run by a Rastafarian who refused to tell me his name.

"What's his problem?" I asked Eric.

"He hates women in the kitchen."

The nighttime sauté guy was also a Rasta. They called him Jah Man. The salad guy, an Indian man with blood-shot eyes, quickly announced, "I'm Bob!"

All of a sudden I heard Eric the Red yell, "Ordering fifteen ribs, ten burgers—five rare, three medium, two well—eight wings, two mussels, two sword, a tuna, three mozz, two guac! Fire eight calamari, six wings!"

The grill man was in a flurry of flipping, dropping, scooping.

"Bring me my vitamins!" he screamed.

Eric the Red had one of the waitresses bring in pitchers of Coke. He poured the Coke into three large paper cups, and he and the Rastas gulped them down. Weeks later, I learned that the Cokes sent to the night boys were mostly rum.

The Amazon waitresses had a rough-and-ready, white-trash charm. They were buxom and petite, which is rare without surgery. They flirted with the line cooks and got fed. The line cooks flirted back and always got their vitamins. It was a package deal. But the waitresses never slept with the cooks. They were after management or the celebrities who came to dance, sip tropical drinks, and be photographed for Page Six, the *New York Post* gossip column.

Page Six, as it turned out, was part of the great PR machine the trio in the trailer was working. They would invite celebs and then feed dirt on them to the gossip columnists. The columnists, like everyone else in the world, loved their jobs being done for them, and everyone was happy.

My first chance to show the Amazon what I had in me came three days after I started. They had a party booked on the beach, the sandy part of the pier that had a volleyball net where drunken models were often coaxed to play. They were expecting two hundred for a sunset beach party.

"Babe! All the A models will be there!" Cornelius said.

I took a look at the menu Eric had written: hot dogs, ribs, burgers. There wasn't much I could do with that. I used kale to garnish the platters, added mango to the salsa, and made a salad out of grilled corn and peppers.

"Wow!" Eric said, watching me add cilantro to the corn. "You're creative."

As he walked to the trailer, he muttered, "I used to be creative . . . then I came here."

One of the models took her top off, and one of the gossip columnists wrote about it. The event was a smash.

The owner of the Amazon was Shimone, a short, stocky, overly tan man with very bad breath. As a new woman on the team, I quickly came to his attention. A petite Russian woman who spent her day in the head trailer counting money for Shimone came to the kitchen one morning: "Shimone would like his usual breakfast, and he would like Rossi to bring it to the trailer."

His usual breakfast was eggs over medium with two whole jalapeños. He would alternate between a bite of jalapeño and a forkful of eggs and then burn it down with strong coffee.

I found him in the trailer with about a hundred grand in bills piled around him.

"I've heard good things, good things . . ."

"Thank you . . . here are your, umm, eggs."

"Tell me, do you need anything here?"

"Well, we need another prep person. The dishwasher is going to quit if he doesn't get a raise. Eric needs a day off. We have to get a fan in the kitchen. We don't have any sharp knives . . ."

Shimone motioned for me to sit, and over the next twenty minutes, he told me the story in detail of how he fought for the Israeli army, was wounded, stitched up his own wound, and crawled back to camp.

"Think of this as a war. You are a soldier."

I looked at him, utterly dumbfounded. Then finally a little voice in the back of my head squeaked out, "Did you make $100,000 a day in the army?"

His eyes grew wide. The Russian woman froze. Shimone was the Napoleon of the Amazon. Only his wife, who we were told was a major investor, talked back to him.

"It will cost you fifty bucks a week to give the dishwasher a raise of a dollar an hour and save us hundreds of dollars training someone new. A decent kitchen fan costs about a hundred, and your team wouldn't need to take as many breaks. Get me another prep person, and I can stop paying Freddy ten dollars an hour to cut celery."

"Okay," he said, suddenly cracking a smile.

"Okay?" I repeated.

"Okay?" the Russian woman repeated, under her breath.

And like that, I was a hero. It took all of ten minutes for the Russian woman to tell the PR trio, the trio to tell the bartenders, the bartenders to tell the bouncers, the bouncers to tell the waitresses, and the waitresses to tell the cooks. By the time the lunch shift began, everyone was smiling at me.

The large bouncer known as Pipe for his habit of calling sex "laying pipe" came into the kitchen.

"You got balls, woman! I'd lay pipe with you in a second, Mama."

"I'll keep that in mind."

Sarah quit in the middle of filleting a twelve-pound salmon.

"I don't blame you," Eric said, and hugged her.

I was quickly promoted to senior sous-chef and catering chef. On Eric's day off, I ran the whole show. The first day I gave the night crew an order, the Rastas walked out.

"We work for Eric," they said.

Eric the Red took me aside. "Screw them. Just tell me what you want, and I'll make sure it happens."

The nighttime grill man was as essential to keeping things running as gas is to a Chevy.

Our dishwasher, Mali, was an African man with ritual scarification marks across his face. Knowing he had allowed someone to cut a mask into his face made the rest of the kitchen keep a healthy distance from him.

On Eric's first day off, I asked Mali to clean the mussels. He looked at me dumbfounded and said nothing.

"Mali?"

"His religion won't allow him to take orders from a woman. It's no disrespect," Badu said softly.

I figured I'd fire Mali, but when I came back into the kitchen, he was cleaning the mussels. After that, when I wanted something from him, I'd yell across the kitchen, "I sure wish someone would clean the calamari!" Then I'd turn my back, so it was as if the air had asked him, not me.

Grandpa was a sweet old man from Ecuador who did the bulk of our prep. He was happy to collect his six dollars an hour and never gave any back talk. We just adored him.

The day Grandpa was shot, things took a decided downturn.

"He'll live," Eric said, rolling up his sleeves to join in as we all made burgers, Grandpa's major job.

It had taken Eric three weeks to train Grandpa, to teach him the proper size and weight of a burger, the perfect slice of calamari, the best celery stick, the way to scrub mussels, to trim chicken breasts, to chop herbs.

I saw it in his eyes as he pressed the burger meat into the mayo lid, pulled it out with Saran Wrap, and started again: Eric had left the building.

After Eric quit, the Russian woman asked me to come to Shimone's trailer.

"Well, I guess, congratulations to you," Shimone said, sipping his espresso. "Or condolences."

"Basically you're asking me to do my job, Eric's job, and Sarah's," I said.

"Is this a problem?"

"Not for the right amount of money."

I asked for three times my pay and demanded to promote internally, hire new cooks, and have free rein to do what I needed to do. Backed into something of a corner, Shimone grunted yes without hesitation.

The Rastas laughed when they heard.

"She won't last a week," the grill man said.

"You're off the schedule. Pick up your check tomorrow," I said, smiling.

"Go home, little girl!" Jah Man yelled.

"You're fired too."

I promoted Badu to head cook, gave Freddy double shifts, and trained Mali to take over Grandpa's chores.

Even Mali started kissing my ass after that.

One morning, Cornelius popped his head into the trailer and said, "Babe, we're doing Vanilla Ice tomorrow. Can you do something extra cool?"

Vanilla Ice's movie had just come out, and all I knew about him was his song "Ice Ice Baby."

I created a buffet of finger food for the Vanilla Ice party: vanilla swordfish kabobs, shrimp on ice, baby vegetables. I thought I was rather clever, but Vanilla arrived wasted and announced he only ate John's pizza or Taco Bell. Didn't matter, the PR trio was so happy they rewarded me by getting famed gossip columnist Richard Johnson to write me up.

"Chef Rossi (even chefs have only one name these

days) went to a lot of trouble preparing items like vanilla swordfish, but Vanilla Ice had John's pizza deliver, which doesn't normally deliver to mortals."

It was my first brush with that elusive thing they call celebrity chef status, and it was intoxicating. After that, the trio promised me tons of mentions in the press, but it never happened again. As it turned out, the trio were champions in getting you one piece of press and then milking it indefinitely.

As the season turned into fall, we found the light at the end of the tunnel. Everyone at the Amazon was running on fumes, but we all knew that once the cold weather came, the outdoor club would have to shut its doors.

The last night, I gave my unofficial permission for everyone to party. The team got their medicine, the floor staff got all the food they wanted, and I got to know that I had survived the most impossible test of whatever I had in me.

I had burn marks on half my upper body. My hair looked like I was sleeping on the street, and my face needed about two hundred facials. But I'd done it. I'd survived the Amazon.

The pier is a kiddie park now. I like walking by and seeing children play. Once I walked to where the kitchen had been. A part of me expected to see one of those hero plaques: "Here stood the valiant crew of the Amazon."

One day, I picked up a handful of sand and considered putting it in my pocket as a keepsake. But that Amazon sand always felt extra dirty. I dumped it and walked away.

# Fried Calamari, Amazon Style

*Serves 4 to 6 people*

### INGREDIENTS
*1 lb. cleaned squid*
*Enough vegetable oil to deep fry in*
*2 coffee cups all-purpose flour*
*Salt and fresh ground pepper*
*½ jar tomato sauce*
*1 lemon, cut into wedges*

### OPTIONAL
*1 pinch oregano*
*1 pinch thyme*

We bought our calamari already cleaned (because can
I just say *yech?*), and then we cut the bodies into half-
inch-thick rings and left the tentacles as is.

We had a deep fryer, but at home you can fill up a deep
pot with three or four inches of vegetable oil for your
own deep fryer.

Heat the oil till it's super hot. You can test this by
dropping almost anything in it and seeing if it bubbles.
Chefs call this the spit test, and I don't even want to talk
about that.

Mix 2 coffee cups of all-purpose flour with salt and
pepper. Toss your calamari in the flour and fry in

batches. Sometimes I like to add dried oregano to this, sometimes I like to add a pinch of dried thyme. Mostly I just leave it super simple. It's done when it's crispy and golden, 1 or 2 minutes. You gotta keep your eye on these, not play with your fancy phone, because calamari gets overcooked super fast, and then it's just a big bowl of rubber bands.

We scooped and dumped our calamari into a bowl, tossed it up with some salt, and served with lemon wedges and a side of tomato sauce, but at home you can drain some of that oil off on paper towels first if you like. Almost any tomato sauce is great for this as a dip. Something simple like marinara is best.

## Swordfish Skewers that Vanilla Ice Wouldn't Eat

*Serves 2 to 3 people*

**INGREDIENTS**

***SWORDFISH***

*1 lb. swordfish, cubed*
*Salt and fresh ground pepper*
*1 drizzle olive oil*

***SAUCE***

*1 coffee cup pineapple juice*
*1 teeny drizzle vanilla extract*
*1 shot heavy cream*
*1 shot coconut milk*
*Salt and fresh ground pepper*
*1 pinch cayenne pepper*

**OPTIONAL**

*1 tablespoon fresh parsley, chopped*
*1 tablespoon fresh cilantro, chopped*
*1 cup pineapple, chopped*

Cut your swordfish into one-inch cubes and season with salt and pepper. Toss in olive oil and lay on a medium-hot grill till well marked on both sides. Let's say 2 minutes per side.

For the sauce, heat up one coffee cup of pineapple juice

with a little itty-bitty drizzle of vanilla extract. Cook for a few minutes, then stir in the heavy cream, coconut milk, and salt and pepper to taste. Cook until the sauce feels like it's getting thick. It should stick to the back of your spoon when you pull it out. I like to add a small pinch of cayenne pepper to this sauce, but it's good as is.

For Vanilla Ice's party, we skewered the cubes, heated them to order, and dunked them in the sauce on their way out the kitchen. You can also top these with fresh chopped parsley or chopped cilantro or add a piece of pineapple to the skewer—word to your mother.

# Provincetown, 1992

I'd been renting a kitchen in a wild nightclub in the East Village called Cave Canem, which means "beware of dog" in Latin. The Cave had been a sensation in the mideighties. Its owner Hayne, a New Orleans debutante turned New York party girl, had turned it into a supper club that featured exotic Roman Empire—style food. By the time I'd discovered the Cave, it had fallen into a rut. New York's elite had abandoned it to a drinking and drugging crowd.

I had a love affair with the huge kitchen, especially the secret passageway that led to another building around the corner. But there were some pitfalls in cooking for such a rough crowd.

In the morning when we walked in to start our prep, we sometimes heard groaning. Looking under the banquette tables, we'd find semiconscious patrons from the night before.

The last straw was the morning we came in to load out for a wedding and found the front entrance to the Cave covered in police tape.

"What happened?" I asked the tiny Filipino janitor in charge of late-night clean up.

"Bouncer get shot in . . . ," and then he put his hand on his crotch.

We had to load the party, watching every step so as not to squish the missing private parts of the nighttime bouncer.

It was time to make a move.

By March of 1992 the corporate catering business, which was booming in the eighties, hit a wall, or rather crashed into one like a torpedo filled with other people's money. Out went Beluga caviar, lobster-tail martinis, and opulent sushi bars. Wall Street yuppies who had been throwing parties chock-full of anything they deemed "ritzy" just to prove how much money they could burn didn't know what had hit them. Their expense accounts went kaput.

After my five-second flirt with fame at the Amazon, I was briefly in demand. It was astounding, really, because I'd been made head chef at the Amazon with no restaurant experience. And, given that I'd helped crank out mediocre food from a camper to thousands of people too drunk to know what they were eating, I still didn't have any.

But my phone was ringing off the hook from folks hoping to cash in on the supper club craze.

I'd been courted by a trio of trust-fund babies to open a supper club in the Flatiron District called Wunderbar. It was supposed to be a Bavarian, nouvelle dance-lounge sensation. Turns out—no surprise here—models and their hangers-on didn't want to eat knockwurst and dance the night away. Wunderbar went underbar. I took the death of both corporate catering budgets and my last restaurant job as a sign from God and decided to follow my sous-chef, Marta, to Provincetown, Massachusetts.

I don't recall how Marta came into my life, but I quickly refused to cater anything without the streetwise Latina lesbian who pulled her long Mohawk into a ponytail. Marta had nothing in the way of manners and everything in the way of passion.

Some chefs took one look at Marta and treated her like a dishwasher—that was, until she stepped into the kitchen. Marta could cook circles around most of the men who crossed her path, but she never called herself a chef.

"Hey man, I'm just a line cook with some extra parsley!" she would say, followed by, "Ain't I pretty?"

Marta decided to take a break from the uppity New York chef scene and moved to Provincetown to chill out. To pay the bills, she took a job flipping burgers at a local bar and grill called Fat Jack's.

She'd found herself a small chicken coop of an apartment behind the L & A Supermarket on Bradford Street, in a string of four such apartments all hidden behind a common, fenced-in front yard. If you kept your head low and sniffed the air for the bay just four blocks away, you could almost pretend you were on the water rather than next to a Dumpster and a pay-by-day parking lot. Marta's place couldn't have been more than four hundred square feet, but it had two floors, and when you counted the lawn furniture in the front yard as your patio, it was livable.

Provincetown, or P-town, is a magical seaside town on the tip of Cape Cod, a Shangri-la for gay people and straight people, for artists and writers and whale watchers and beachcombers and drag queens and blue-haired old ladies and leather boys and happy children—anyone who wants to create, escape, or embrace life.

Marta coerced her landlord into renting me the smallest chicken coop, right next to hers. It was maybe two hundred square feet, with no second floor. The tiny bathroom was in the kitchen, so close to the stove you could actually stir a sauce and wash your hair at the same time. The ceiling in the bathroom was just a piece of plastic over exposed insulation. If I agreed to drag the garbage cans out to the curb for the tenants twice a week, I could have the tiny pad for four hundred bucks a month.

Marta hauled me out there in her beat-up jalopy, Mabel. Our six-hour drive, which turned into eight with traffic, was graced with eleven boxes of my crap and my two fat, crying cats. Did I mention I get carsick?

I got a cheap futon mattress from somebody leaving town and put that on my scratched-up wooden floor. I hopped to a few garage sales and found a wicker chair, a set of dresser drawers, a small table that would serve as a desk, and two beach chairs.

Those days, nobody had a computer. I wrote via an electric typewriter. I ran an extension cord to the front lawn and set my typewriter up on the little table I'd bought. Then I unfolded a beach chair, and voilà: instant outdoor writer's studio, one that needed three layers of clothing and a down coat to use. It was March, after all.

I set up my easel and paints near the front window, but even though I was in an artist's oasis, I didn't feel the pull of the brush. The pen called to me instead.

Provincetown in March is a haunting and beautiful place. On a stroll down Commercial Street, you would barely bump into a dozen strollers. It's a far cry from bustling July when the street gets so packed with tourists that they have to block it off to traffic.

The only places open in March were Fat Jack's; Nappy's, a local, eclectic restaurant off the main drag that was run by an ex-hippie type; a fancier joint called the Mews that doled out pricey food but kept its quality consistent so folks didn't bitch about it; the liquor store; and the A-House. The A-House was a sleazy, nautical-themed nightclub for gay boys. I'd heard Billie Holiday once sang there. It was a great place for a drink, but women weren't exactly welcome.

Marta and I would drive Mabel to the A & P, about a mile from our chicken coops, and load up on groceries. We did our cooking coop to coop. My kitchen would make the salad and pasta. Her kitchen would make the chicken and the tomato sauce. Marta's diverse music collection accompanied our dinners. She'd put about ten dollars into fixing up her apartment and about two thousand into her sound system. A typical Marta mix might start with Aretha Franklin, rock into Led Zeppelin, cruise into Cuban jazz, and then boogie over to seventies disco.

"Hey man, I like my tunes!" she would yell, popping

the lid off another Rolling Rock, which she liked to call "Rolling Cock."

Sometimes we'd drive down Bradford Street all the way to the ocean, park Mabel at Herring Cove Beach, and watch the sunset. The salty smell of the ocean put a warm buzzing feeling into my solar plexus that I could never quite explain. Growing up on the Jersey Shore, I'd always lived smelling distance from the ocean, and getting near it made me feel like I was crawling back into the womb. One whiff and it was like I'd taken a happy pill. Marta would throw rocks in the water and kick her feet in the sand, but not me. I'd just stand there, close my eyes, and smell.

Marta hated the owner of Fat Jack's. She said he treated her like trash. The town was starving for anything ethnic, and Marta had suggested a Cuban night, honoring her family recipes. "We need some ropa vieja and some tostones! Rapido Papi!" It had gone over like a stink bomb. Seriously. I think the man held his nose. Marta said the darling little seaside town that accepted men walking down the street wearing nothing but leather chaps and a jockstrap was not so forgiving to those with a little color in their skin.

"Look around, man! You see anyone chocolate? Ain't no doors open to me in this town!"

I didn't see P-town that way, and not just because I didn't have her caramel skin. P-town was the first time I had let my breath out in more than a decade.

In the eleven-year span that included running away from home, surviving Crown Heights, becoming a bartender who was morphing into a chef, and moving into a Manhattan apartment so dangerous that the week after I moved in my upstairs neighbor was stabbed to death in his bathtub—I hadn't slowed down enough to realize I was running.

As cramped as my chicken coop was, it was safe. People in P-town didn't even lock their doors. When strange noises went bump in the night, they weren't from gang members roughing someone up or shootings or sirens or screams. They were feral cats getting into fights or a raccoon digging in the garbage or a drunken drag queen singing Liza Minnelli.

Phooosh! It was like I could float.

A month of fun and relaxation was marvelous. Even the way I looked changed. My eyes lost their dark circles and my shoulders eased down to their proper place instead of up around my ears, but by late April I was starting to get antsy. A girl can only chill out for so long. Well, a New York girl, anyway.

There was a mag in town called *Provincetown Magazine*. It was a freebie largely dedicated to advertisements, but it did have an article or three. I knocked on the office door and was greeted by a blond woman named Tina who looked as though she'd spent some time on a softball field. Behind her was a quiet, bespectacled little woman who looked like a librarian. Her name was Anne.

I had just purchased my first pair of black biker boots at the leather joint in town. I was filled with so much abandon from not having to worry about getting mugged every time I came home that everything felt like cause for celebration. It was a warm April day, and I wore my mid-calf harness boots with cutoff jeans, a Blondie T-shirt, and a worn jean jacket. My hair, as always, was a blond pile of curl and frizz. I thought I looked super cool, but looking back, I probably looked like a loony who just fell off the back of a motorcycle. Luckily, the ladies thought I was a breath of fresh air.

"Love your boots!" Tina said as I walked in the door.

"Yes, yes, they are very unusual worn that way," Anne stammered. "You know, with shorts!"

Within twenty minutes, I had a cooking column.

My first column was a thousand words, one full page. I wrote about the recipes I invented when my mother abandoned real cooking. A week later, I picked up a copy of the magazine and saw my name in print for the first time. It felt like a gold star.

I clipped the column and mailed it to my mom, thinking she might like to see my first published bit of writing but also worried she'd be mad I was poking fun at her.

She called a week later. She'd made thirty copies and mailed them to all our relatives.

"Shana Madelah, you have immortalized me!" she screamed.

Mom and I hadn't exactly been the best of friends after she and my dad had dumped me on the Hasids, but she'd had a severe stroke that had left her partially paralyzed. Seeing her in a wheelchair had really killed the anger I'd been hanging on to. She slurred her words and couldn't use her left hand. It was pretty hard to be anything but sweet to her. We started to talk on the phone every week.

She'd been a frustrated poet and felt thrilled to live vicariously through my writing accomplishments.

"Slovah Davida Shana!" My mother loved calling me by my Yiddish name, which Eastern European yentas like my mother often preferred to plant on their children rather than a more classic Hebrew name like Sarah. She said it meant "beautiful daughter of David." They were trying to name me Sarah and David at the same time; no wonder my sexuality got a little confused.

"Promise to keep writing about me!"

"Mom, how could I not? There's so much material!"

So, every Wednesday when the new mag came out, I would cut out my column and mail it to Mom. She would make my dad drive her to the drugstore for two dozen copies and mail them to a slew of distant cousins, aunts, and uncles whom I hadn't seen since I was four.

"Mom . . . I don't even know them!"

"If they throw it out, they throw it out! A mother has a right to kvell!"

I pretended to be annoyed, but living on my own, I had met some terrifying challenges. After every mountain I climbed, there was no one on the other side applauding. I came to understand just how rare it is to have someone so proud of you they want to share your accomplishments with the world.

"Okay, Mom, whatever you want, but stop mailing me Wendy's coupons will ya? They don't even have fast food places out here."

# Ropa Vieja

*Serves 4 to 6 people*

**INGREDIENTS**
*3 carrots, chopped*
*3 onions, chopped*
*4 garlic cloves, sliced*
*A few good drizzles olive oil*
*1 pinch smoked chili powder*
*2 (28 oz.) cans crushed tomatoes*
*Salt and fresh ground pepper*
*2 bay leaves*
*2 lbs. flank steak*
*2 plum tomatoes, julienned*
*½ red onion, julienned*
*1 each red bell pepper, green bell pepper, and jalapeño, julienned*
*1 handful fresh cilantro, chopped*

Sauté carrots, onion, and garlic in olive oil over medium high heat for 5 minutes. Punch it up with a pinch of smoked chili powder.

Cook for a minute then add crushed tomatoes and any liquid left in the can. Add salt and pepper to taste.

Bring to a boil, add the bay leaves and the meat, and reduce heat to a simmer.

Cook covered for 3 hours.

Pull the meat out and let cool just enough to handle and then shred by hand. It should fall apart easily, like my love life.

Strain your sauce and put aside.

Sauté julienned plum tomato, red onion, bell pepper, and jalapeño, and after about 5 minutes or so (when the veggies are soft and have color) throw in the meat and strained sauce. Cook for one minute.

Add fresh chopped cilantro, adjust salt and pepper, and you are done! Serve with Mellow Yellow Rice.

# Mellow Yellow Rice

*Serve wih Ropa Vieja*

### INGREDIENTS

*3 coffee cups water, vegetable stock, or chicken stock*
*1 good pinch saffron or turmeric*
*A couple pinches salt*
*2 coffee cups uncooked long grain white rice*
*1 shot olive oil*
*1 pinch ground cumin*

### OPTIONAL

*Goya Sazón*
*Peas*
*Pimientos*

Boil water, vegetable stock, or chicken stock with a good pinch of saffron or turmeric, and salt to taste.

In a deep, heavy-bottom pot, sauté rice in olive oil over medium heat. Add a generous pinch of ground cumin and salt. Cook for a few minutes. Add your boiling liquid and bring to a boil, then boil for 3 minutes.

Lower heat to medium and cook covered (with a tight fitting lid so no steam escapes) for 7 minutes.

Turn off heat and leave covered for 15 minutes.

It's hard not to open the lid and check along the way, but if you slap your own wrists and leave that lid alone, it will work out just fine.

This will get you nice firm rice. If you like your rice a little softer, add another shot or two of liquid.

Sometimes I like to add Goya's Sazón seasoning instead of the spices. Sometimes I add peas or pimientos, but when I am serving it with Ropa Vieja, I just leave it as is. The Ropa has enough veggies for both.

# The Last Sunset

Being a woman who wears harness boots with shorts and writes a column in a small local magazine wouldn't even warrant a smile in New York City, but in P-town in April, I was suddenly a very big, blond fish in a very small, quirky pond.

Businesses were starting to open for the season, at least on weekends. It was like watching Provincetown wake from a long nap. A local gym invited me to bake healthy cookies for them to sell for a dollar. A gourmet market asked me to make gazpacho and pasta salad.

I was bouncing back and forth, using Marta's oven to bake the cookies, my stove to boil the pasta, typing articles on the front lawn. Suddenly, I felt busier than I had been in Manhattan.

Marta began to close her door at night instead of leaving it open for me to pop in whenever I wanted to, uninvited. I could hear James Brown and Mick Jagger blaring out her window. The afternoons when I came by to bake cookies, she would stay upstairs until I was done.

"What gives?" I yelled up the stairs one day.

She yelled down, "Mi hijita, Mami, you been here two months and you got a cooking column, everyone wants your food, everyone loves you. I been here a year, and nobody offers me shit. It's all because you're a honky!"

No matter how hard I tried to make things right, nothing eased her frustration. She discovered that some of her pals were making a nice living selling crafts at a large flea market in Wellfleet, so she quit her job at Fat Jack's and started making trips to New York City, loading up on African statues and jewelry and selling the trinkets at the market.

"If they're gonna see me as Shaka Zulu, I'm gonna sharpen my spear!"

She adorned herself in African beads and pendants, wore dashikis, and actually made a lot more money selling beads on the weekends than she ever had burning herself over the grill at Fat Jack's.

But our friendship was never the same.

One day, after I'd typed up the week's cooking column, I walked over to the magazine to drop it off. Anne the librarian was at the desk. After complimenting me on my boots, again, she asked me out to dinner. I didn't know much about her, but Tina had told me Anne was straight. I figured she was just being friendly.

After Marta had pulled away from me, I'd been having dinners alone. I tried to fill the vacant space that had been filled with Marta's wondrous, cackling laughter by eating, but making pasta for one felt wrong. Pasta is like a bottle of wine. It demands company.

Anne and I went to Franco's on the Bay a few days later. I have a vague recollection of eating cod in some sort of caper sauce, but mostly what I remember was laughing for hours. On the long walk down Commercial Street that night, we wound up kissing. Turns out the librarian wasn't so straight after all.

I have seen many transformations in my life, but Anne's was so startling because *I* was the catalyst.

Within two weeks of the start of our affair, she cut her long, limp hair into a hip, androgynous 'do, stopped wearing slacks and button-down shirts, and started wearing jeans with big tomboy belts, black T-shirts, and leather ankle boots. One day in the parking lot of the Laundromat, she and I danced the hustle for the entertainment of the dozen people folding their clothes.

The shy secretaryish caterpillar turned into a dancing, singing rock 'n' roll butterfly.

I don't know what shocked people more: that Anne was opening up so dramatically or that she was dating a woman.

The problem with P-town off-season is that it's a small town—a small town with a long memory. Ever after, I was known as the New York girl who had coerced Anne into vacating her heterosexuality. I wanted to be known as the chef writer, not the great corrupter of women!

When the high season of summer descended on P-town, I had to give up my quiet oasis of friendly hellos and long chats on the bay beach. Suddenly, thousands of people filled the streets, performers handed out advertisements for their shows, drag queens paraded in front of the night-clubs, there were no parking spots to be had, and when I passed someone I knew, they were always in too much of a rush to talk.

But inside my fence I typed away, turning out columns for the magazine. My wheat-free cookies were selling nicely at the gym, and my gazpacho was a big hit at the gourmet market. I started to get catering work too and even coerced Marta into abandoning her beads and anger long enough to help me crank out great food for rich lesbians one night. My reward after a productive day of writing and cooking was waiting four blocks away, at the bay.

At the end of the day, after the sunbathers, dog walkers, and screaming children had gone, I walked the scraggle of beach that curves around Provincetown Harbor, inhaling the brine and diesel and sweet, rotting seaweed.

There is a majesty to the town's oceanside beaches, but the little bay beach has a haunting beauty as the sun sets. The rickety piers, ramshackle cottages, and relics of fishing boats past their prime are cast into an ash silhouette, and then, for an inexplicable instant, a brilliant light erupts and paints the scene a magical white. Locals claim this light as their own. It's lured generations of artists, but few have captured it—that one last supernatural burst of glory before the outermost tip of the world swallows the sun.

I felt as though I was cheating on the ocean with the bay, but I gotta say, it pulled at my heartstrings just as strong.

By the time I got used to the hustle-bustle of Province-town's high season, Labor Day was upon us. The four-day weekend is a mass party of drunken young lesbians, dancing gay boys making the most of their last weekend to wear white, happy tourists munching on fresh breads from the Portuguese bakery, and artists hiding from them all on the bay beach, trying to paint those aging fishing boats one last time.

And then it was over. Autumn was approaching, and with it, the end of my lease and the call of catering back in New York City. A wedding I'd catered the previous year had spread the word about me to a slew of the happy couple's cronies, and my life as a wedding caterer was start-ing to form. I had a large wedding on September 19 in Long Island City. It was time to leave Shangri-la.

The irony of that summer was that my cooking col-umn had brought Mom and I closer, but living on Cape Cod also brought the longest stretch I'd ever gone without seeing her: nine months. I was planning on visiting my folks at our family home in Jersey for a Rosh Hashanah reunion, but as I was getting ready to leave town with my rental truck full of crap and two screaming cats, my dad called to say that they had decided to drive to Florida to check on their real estate.

"We'll still see each other when we get back to Rumson for Rosh Hashanah," he said.

Mom was in the background screaming, clearly in the throes of one of her "five million ways to save money" fits.

Today's topic was why the coupons for the Wendy's salad bar were better than the coupons at McDonald's—because Wendy's was all you can eat.

"Do you want to talk to your mother?" Dad asked, sounding exhausted.

"Nah. She sounds too crazy today. Tell her I'll talk to her when she gets back to Jersey."

The librarian and I promised each other that we'd keep our romance going, long distance. Neither one of us said what most of our friends knew: it was a summer fling and should be left that way.

During my last few days in town, I walked along the bay beach trying to suck in every bit of the funk and the beauty I could. I walked up and down Commercial Street saying goodbye to every friendly face, and as the sun set, I sat on the concrete wall overlooking the bay at St. Mary's Church, kissing Anne and pretending that it wasn't all going to end.

I was twenty-eight years old and couldn't shake the feeling that the moment I left town, my life as a young woman was over. I wasn't entirely wrong.

Soon after I got back to New York, I transformed my half-assed attempt at having my own business into running a bona fide catering company, with the stress, employees, and rent to go with it. My carefree days were about to float away in a sea of canapés.

I moved to Chelsea on a Thursday. By Monday it felt as if I'd been back in the city for a year.

What I remember most about catering that first wedding after returning to New York on September 19, 1992, was that something was off with me all day. I snapped at my dishwasher over a small bit of grease left in a bowl. My normally beautifully decorated hors d'oeuvre trays looked flat and uninspired. My kitchen staff looked at me and shook their heads as I made a mess out of everything I tried to slice. I thought it was just angst over not being in P-town.

When it came time to cut the three-tiered wedding cake, my chef Badu took the knife out of my hand. I was hacking at the bottom layer as if I had an ice pick.

"Go sit down," he said, "before you kill someone."

At 2:00 a.m. I returned to my dark apartment building, took the elevator to my studio, and once inside, threw my bag on the parquet floor. I noticed the red light blinking on my answering machine and pressed play.

I heard my dad's voice.

"I'm so sorry to leave this on your machine . . . Your mother and I were driving back from Florida, and she started to not feel well in North Carolina. So we went to a hospital and . . . she died."

I hadn't been home long enough to load up on groceries or wine, but I recalled there was a beer left in the fridge. I flipped the top off and drank it in three swallows. Something inside of me that I was not ready for was about to erupt.

I'd found a small bit of sand in the cuff of my Levi's. I poured it carefully into a teacup and left it on the coffee table. I collapsed onto my couch and raked my index finger through that sand. Then I closed my eyes and tried to remember what the bay smelled like.

*Marty, Harriet, and their demon seed (1981).*

# Harriet's Turkey and Rice Meatballs

*Serves 4 to 8 people*

There were a few things Mom was still willing to cook even after she discovered the microwave. One was her turkey and rice meatballs. I think it's because she wanted to eat them as much as we did.

Having discovered that I was allergic to wheat in my adult years, I've come to feel super appreciative of bread-crumbless meatballs.

As a chef and a caterer, I naturally have tried to improve on Mom's recipe by making my own tomato sauce, browning the turkey balls before I boiled them, and mixing in turkey sausage, but in the end I always come back to Mom's way, store-bought marinara sauce and all.

**INGREDIENTS**
*2 lbs. ground turkey*
*1½ coffee cups white rice, uncooked*
*1 pinch paprika*
*2 pinches dried oregano*
*2 pinches garlic powder*
*1 pinch salt and fresh ground pepper*
*2 eggs, beaten*
*2 (16 oz.) jars tomato sauce (Mom liked Ragu)*

Start out with 2 lbs. of ground turkey 'cause you want to make enough for a crowd. Then invite me over please!

Meanwhile, prepare about a coffee cup and a half of uncooked white rice however you like to cook it, so long as it's plain and simple.

Mix your turkey and your cooked white rice with a pinch of paprika, 2 pinches of dried oregano, 2 pinches of garlic powder, and a pinch each of salt and pepper. Pour in 2 beaten eggs, and mix the whole shebang well. Then form into balls.

Pour a good amount of tomato sauce, let's say 2 (16 oz.) jars, in a deep pot and bring to a boil. Add your balls and reduce to a simmer. Then cover the pot and cook until your meat is totally cooked through, about a half hour or so should do it. If the meatballs are not submerged in sauce, add a few shots of water or a little more sauce until they are.

Mom served these over spaghetti, but they are killer as is. My favorite way to eat Mom's turkey balls was cold out of the fridge the next day.

# Ross by Way of Goldstein

My mother's last name wasn't Goldstein. It wasn't Gold-blatt, Lowenstein, or Lefkowitz either. It was Ross. Well, actually, Ross was her married name. Harriet Ruby Gross was her maiden name. I gotta say I went through high school feeling extremely grateful that Gross wasn't *my* last name.

After school, Mom would try to feed us some horrifying relic from the Old Country, like kishke. Not the Old Country where she was born, which was New Jersey, but the Old Country of her parents, Hungary.

Don't even get me started on kishke; I think it's cow intestine stuffed with potatoes, chicken fat, and assorted meat parts. I don't really want to know, because, you see, I've eaten kishke.

She also applied kishke (the term, not the actual intestines) to the region below the belly button and above the groin. "MOM, that's really gross!" we would say, to which she would reply, "Don't say 'gross'! That's a lovely Jewish name, and now they ruined it!"

"They" also made the lovely pine trees Christian by

anointing them as Christmas trees. "They have to take everything nice and make it GOY!" Mom would announce every Christmas season.

But I digress.

I'd grown up thinking my dad's name was shortened when his father came through Ellis Island. I didn't find out until I was well into my twenties that out of twelve brothers and sisters, only my dad and a big brother he idolized had shortened the family name from Rosenthal to Ross. They were both businessmen and didn't want to suffer the wrath of anti-Semitism that swept this country in the fifties.

The name Ross never suited me. Far too normal, I suspect, but it worked fine after an "I" was added, to make Rossi, my then first and later only name. Folks tend to think I'm Italian until I drop one too many "oys."

Harriet Ruby Ross sounds like an intellectual or a politician or a mathematician or a poet or, perhaps, a musician. In fact, my mother was all of those things. She so excelled in school that she jumped grades, graduating high school at fourteen. She went on to get her master's degree, not so common for working-class women in the forties. She taught everything from grammar school to college. When I was ten, I discovered my mother's greatest career highlight.

One afternoon, I pulled out a large, black photo album in the basement and flicked through photos of dead relatives until I came upon a happy, dancing Albert Einstein at what appeared to be my parents' wedding!

When I asked my mom about it, she replied, "Oh, I

was one of his lab assistants." When I acted impressed, she replied, "Slovah, it's nothing. He had twenty-four lab assistants."

Mom explained that Mr. Einstein was an adorable, sweet Jewish man who was so absentminded that he had a housekeeper who followed him around and not only reminded him to eat but also reminded him to use the bathroom. Mom said when Albert's head was in the clouds, he might easily have anointed himself if his housekeeper hadn't reminded him to go to the toilet.

It was clear by the way she spoke about Einstein that she was very fond of him, which made it even stranger that she'd never mentioned working under the greatest mind of his century, and yet spent countless hours bragging about her less-than-perfect children and their every minute accomplishment. My getting an A- in history meant a round of phone calls to aging relatives about her brilliant daughter. My brother Matt actually hitting the ball in Little League meant letters to France and postcards to California. Mom working for Albert Einstein— not a peep!

She played the violin at one point with an orchestra that I recall was the New Jersey Symphony Orchestra but may well have been the Monmouth Symphony Orchestra. She wrote poetry, including one piece that won a contest and was written up in a local paper. She was a brilliant mathematician and college professor and spoke Yiddish, German, French, and English. She put my dad through law school by teaching and so loved her job that my dad, seeing the joy in her eyes compared with the torment

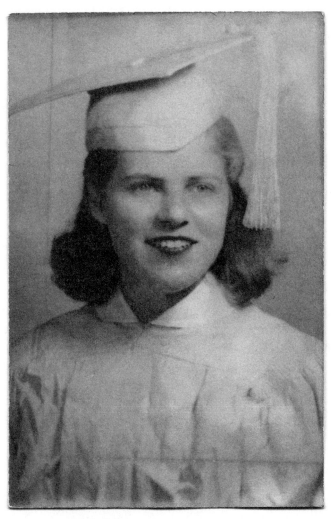

*My mom's college graduation (1948).*

that was his career as an attorney, quit law and became a sixth-grade teacher. Not a great career move, you might say, but it gave them the summers off to travel around the country, and this they did enthusiastically right up until the end.

Although Mom married when she was twenty-six, she didn't have her first kid till she was thirty-six. She had eight miscarriages, tried to adopt, and admitted to me that she had even considered buying a baby on the black market. Only after she lay in bed for nine months, like Sophia Loren, was her first baby, my sister Lillian, born. Lily was premature, needed to be incubated, and had to wear braces on her legs for her early years, but she lived.

At thirty-eight, Mom had me. I shot out at over ten pounds, healthy, happy, and hungry. She said the doctor only needed a catcher's mitt. I demanded to be fed the moment I hit open air. My brother was born with some difficulty a year and a half later, but he made it just fine. My mother was forty years old at this point, not so common for new mothers in the sixties. She'd been her hometown beauty queen but had put on so much weight lying in bed for three pregnancies that she just gave up and kept eating.

After the trauma of eight miscarriages, Mom gave up her career, her beautiful figure, and her mathematical studies. She still plucked her violin occasionally and wrote poetry that had an innocent, childlike quality, but other than that, she dedicated herself heart, body, and soul to watching over her children like a mother hen . . . on acid.

My brother, sister, and I were alternately suffocated and lovingly protected by Mom, the kvelling hen.

So while I sit in awe of all the accomplishments of overachiever Harriet Ruby Gross Ross, I never knew that woman.

The woman who raised me was Harriet, the larger-than-life Yiddish mama who saved more money on coupons than most people make in a lifetime, who could scold you in four languages—sometimes at the same time—who believed that if her children visited a church, they would be ruined the same way Easter ruined hard-boiled eggs.

I remember the day I was reaching just a little too far into the oven to retrieve a tray of fish sticks (fish sticks had their own food group in my household), and my mother screamed, "Slovah, while you're in the oven . . . "

"Mom!"

"Slovah, I want you to know that if you ever eat pork, you'll smell your ancestors burning!"

"Mom!"

"Your great-great-and-many-more-greats-grandfather was burned at the stake by Queen Isabella for refusing to eat pork in front of his congregation."

"Mom, we're Hungarian, not Spanish!"

My mother smiled her usual "you'll see" smile and went back to slicing a head of iceberg lettuce into large, flavorless, pale green rings. To this day, I am sure that the sole purpose for the existence of iceberg lettuce is to give Jewish mothers something to do while torturing their children.

At a cocktail party many years later, I found myself

in the midst of a semidrunken chat with a young woman who had just earned her PhD in anthropology. Her specialty? Hungary.

"Why, it makes perfect sense that your family might have suffered in the Spanish Inquisition. The flight to Eastern Europe was a common one for Jews escaping Spain. To wind up in Hungary was fairly normal."

"You mean my mom was telling the truth?" I said a little louder than I'd intended.

"Well, yeah, probably . . . but I don't think there's a lot of stock to her somehow knowing you are the direct descendant of King David."

"Guess that shoots the hell out of the second half of that speech."

"Which is . . . "

"That I carry the seed of the Messiah."

Oh yeah, that little ditty was a potent one. Mom reminded my sister and me on a monthly basis that since we were, in fact, direct descendants of King David, as in "David and Goliath" David, we might carry the future offspring who just might parent the future Messiah or even the Messiah himself! So were we to hang a little too closely with Christian boys, we could, ya know . . . poison the line and therefore destroy the chance of the savior being born and all that.

Rather heavy for an eight-year-old, I can assure you.

A few years after the cocktail party with the anthropologist, I met a Hungarian filmmaker.

"My mom tried to convince us that our family came

from Transylvania," I said, jokingly. "I think it was one Dracula movie too many."

"Well, actually, some of Satmar and the surrounding area that your family comes from has now been eaten up by Romania, and Transylvania is in that area. So, you know, your mom might just be right about your clan coming from Dracula-ville."

I blurted the only response I could muster: "OY!"

My mother is the only person I have ever met who missed me while I was still in the room. She also taught me that laughing at life was often the best way to get through it and that there was only half joy in paying full price.

"Harriet Ross" simply doesn't fit this woman, and so I decided to give my mother a new name. Why, you ask? . . . Why not? (Jewish women always answer a question with another question.)

So for all those in earshot, I shout out loud and proud, I am Harriet Ruby Gross Ross Goldstein's daughter!

Now I have to go. With all this excitement, my kishkes are killing me.

# Harriet's Roast Chicken

*Serves 4 to 6 people*

### INGREDIENTS
*1 whole chicken, cut up by a butcher (Mom got kosher, of course)*
*1 pinch each garlic powder, paprika, dried oregano, fresh ground pepper, and salt if you like it (Mom didn't use it)*
*1 drizzle olive oil*

### OPTIONAL
*Coffee cup apple juice*
*Coffee cup orange juice*

The only seasonings I ever saw in our home were oregano, garlic powder, and paprika, sometimes the odd salt-and-pepper packet taken from a fast food restaurant, but Mom's roast chicken was a crowd pleaser.

She'd start with a whole chicken cut up by the butcher because cutting up a chicken yourself? Not so fun!

Some folks wash the chicken first. That's smart, but Mom always got kosher chicken, which had already been brined so she wouldn't have to.

She'd plop the chicken in a big bowl and toss with garlic powder, paprika, oregano, and pepper. Mom didn't use salt, but I'm going to suggest that you do. You want just enough seasoning to cover the chicken well. Then you drizzle on oil and mish it all up.

Preheat the oven to 350 and lay out all your parts on a roasting pan and . . . roast. Normally, an hour would do it, but my family liked our food to be fall-off-the-bone done, so Mom would leave it in for about an hour and a half. Once the chicken has color and is getting crispy, you can turn the oven down to 300. If at any point the chicken starts to look dry, baste with the juices. Mom liked to pour in some water, but I am partial to orange juice or apple juice.

Now, once your chicken is crispy on the outside and soft on the inside, it's done. You can just pour the pan juices over it and devour. But to tell the truth, no one in my family liked this dish half as much when it was cooked as we did the next day, cold from the fridge. Oh my lord, that was fun to pick at!

So in honor of Harriet, cook your chicken, but don't serve it! Put it in the fridge and eat it the next day cold, dipped in mustard. OY VEY, is that good!

# Wedding Caterer Blues

That wedding I was catering on September 19, 1992—the night my mother died—was at the Metropolitan Building, an old electrical-parts factory turned into a party space and movie-shoot venue by a spectacularly eclectic woman named Eleanor. I've lived a lifetime of befriending odd-balls, but I have to say that Eleanor is the most eccentric woman I have ever known.

A tall woman in her sixties, she dressed in frocks and robes that made her look like a Chinese emperor or a Middle Eastern sheikh.

She offered to let me use her kitchen for free in exchange for my catering the building's events. It seemed like a dream-come-true deal.

When I first started to cook there, Eleanor would arrive to work in a sidecar attached to a motorcycle driven by a pal of hers. She also had a seventies limousine with a full bar in the back and would have her head maintenance man, a somber, middle-aged guy named Juan, drive her around in the limo while she drank scotch in the back.

The Metro is a gorgeous industrial building, filled with mismatched antiques, sandblasted brick walls, chandeliers, and a cage-style elevator that takes guests from the concrete loading dock of a desolate industrial street to the chic party space inside.

Back then, it was a diamond in the rough, and I do mean rough. The ceiling leaked and the floors creaked. A slew of prostitutes congregated outside, and sometimes, just as the bride and groom were saying their "I dos," they would scream something like, "I'll stab you, Laacreeesha!"

Cooking at the Metro was a challenge. It had something of a country kitchen, with one beaten-up old stove that had only two temperatures: cold and nuclear. The refrigeration unit seemed to be held together with Juan's bubble gum.

The building had become a darling of off-kilter film shoots. I never knew whom I might find rummaging through my food. It didn't matter that we'd plaster the refrigerator with masking tape on which was scrawled "Do Not Touch!"

One week while I was cooking for a bar mitzvah, I looked up to see a woman with a spectacularly long neck staring at me. "That's Linda Lovelace," one of my prep cooks whispered.

She had a sore throat that day and was wrapped in a blanket sipping tea with honey. I was so absorbed by the realization that I was watching the seventies porn legend from *Deep Throat* nurse a sore throat that I didn't notice the camera crew had stolen half the shrimp I'd been poaching. Just another day at the Metro.

Having a kitchen allowed me the freedom to really expand my catering business, and I quickly outgrew the Metro and moved into a huge industrial warehouse turned commercial kitchen in Long Island City.

It wasn't as though I sat down and decided to become a wedding caterer. It's just that I started catering weddings in the late eighties, and my brides and grooms wouldn't stop talking about me. Then I catered their friends' and families' weddings in the nineties, and they told their friends and families, too. By the time we edged into the millennium, I was officially known as one of New York City's wildest wedding caterers.

To be a good wedding caterer, it certainly helps to know how to cook, but to be perfectly honest, a psychotherapy license might be more useful.

I have seen it all, my dears—the bride who asked that I promise her that her wedding would continue were I killed in a car accident. She wanted it in an addendum to her catering contract.

Then there was the bride who called me every day for the year leading up to her wedding, sometimes I think just to make sure I had not run off to Mexico with her deposit.

If you can't be a psychotherapist, it wouldn't hurt to be a former secretary of state. For instance, when the bride's father is no longer speaking to the bride's mother (if he ever was to begin with) and the groom's brother owes the groom's best man money he'll never see again, it takes a superhuman ability to instill enough Zen to get these folks to huddle together for a half hour of family photos so that the food can go out while it's still edible.

Despite what anyone says, catering is anything but glamorous.

How 'bout taking a little walk in my shoes for a typical wedding weekend in the late nineties?

Friday morning: I attempt to answer all the phone inquiries that came in Thursday night before taking a car service to my kitchen in Long Island City.

I call back two bar mitzvah moms, three brides, and one set of in-laws, then I pick up bagels and Coke (the soda kind) for my kitchen crew, and hop a cab uptown to the Fifty-Ninth Street Bridge.

Bagels and cola are a must for pro cooks, second only to strong coffee and cigarettes. Ask anyone.

My large warehouse turned commercial kitchen felt a bit like the Batcave. You could drive a truck into this spacious kitchen, but you couldn't buy a stick of butter anywhere in the neighborhood. Back then, Long Island City was a no-man's-land, far from the developed hipster darling it is today. LIC was a fifteen-minute drive from my apartment in the East Village when there was no traffic, but during Manhattan rush hour, you could write a novel as you plugged along.

As I walk into the warehouse kitchen, I find my sous-chef, Shimi, pacing back and forth along the fifty feet of stainless-steel tables that constituted our assembly line. He keeps looking at the clock and repeating his Friday morning mantra: "Where is he? Where is he?"

"He" is the meat and fish man, who has the best product for the best price but is always, always late.

"We've got nothing to do till he gets here. Nothing!"

"Hmmm," I say in my subtle, Oh-really-well-what-about-these-bazillion-little-things voice. "I'm sure there are a few things we can do."

I point to the items on the prep list taped to the walk-in refrigerator door that have nothing to do with meat and fish: roast and peel a half case of red bell peppers, dice twenty white onions, roast two cases of beets, wash and quarter one hundred pounds of Yukon gold potatoes then soak them in buckets of water, clean and cut one case of fennel . . .

"Just a few things."

Niko is smiling and cutting up eighty pounds of cheese, labeling each batch, using his unique language skills. Smoked Gouda is marked "Goda." The aluminum tin of sharp English cheddar has been identified as "Cheater."

"Relax . . . everything is fine . . . life is fine," Niko says in his Slovenian accent. He is always serene in a way common to both truly spiritual people and serial killers.

I look over at the tall, bearded man that everyone thinks is Russian. I had lost my darling Adam. Marta had driven away in a fume of resentment. The Big S got so busy running the catering operation for a racetrack in San Diego that she stopped coming to New York City. She also lost a hundred pounds on Atkins and we had to change her name to the Little S. Shimi, my sous-chef, had about as much interest in improving his cooking skills as I did in learning ballet. Niko entering my life was like hitting the culinary jackpot. Here was a talented, hard-working chef who didn't mind taking orders from a woman and had a total potty mouth. WIN!

I push my mess of hair under a bandanna and put on a chef jacket that I swim in like a giant muumuu. We asked once for a few extra-large chef jackets, and the linen company sent nothing but elephant-size jackets ever after.

We get into it.

I squeeze a pint of fresh lemon juice and wash a kilo of cilantro, then toast a handful of ground cumin in a dry pan for the cilantro chutney.

Niko rolls logs of goat cheese in fresh rosemary and cracked black pepper then wraps them in plastic wrap.

Shimi takes in deliveries . . . and complains.

Our Ecuadoran dishwasher and prep person smiles, cleans twenty bunches of parsley, and goes to her happy place, where she will be lost in her faraway thoughts for hours on end. Periodically, she looks at us and says, in her little bit of English, "Ya, ya . . . ya."

The meat and fish man finally shows up. He says what he always says: "Traffic on the bridge."

The delivery looks like the morgue released two bodies. A coffin-size Styrofoam box containing one hundred pounds of whole salmon filet is unloaded into the bottom shelf of the walk-in. Two leaking cardboard boxes containing 180 pieces of chicken breast are placed on the metal shelf by the sink while our dishwasher scurries to bleach the hundred-foot trail of chicken juice running from the door to the sink.

"Would it kill you to put these boxes in a garbage bag?"

I scream at the meat and fish man on his way out. He gives me the finger.

Shimi and Niko start cutting off the tenders and putting them aside for chicken stock, then trimming the extra fat from the chicken breasts. It takes them an hour and a half. The dishwasher starts dicing the twenty pounds of onion.

The salmon has been ordered "all the way," which means it's supposed to have no skin and no bones, but owing to a life-long fear of fish bones in my throat, I have Niko examine the fish for pin bones to pull out with tweezers. He finds them on every slab of fish.

We roast the excess chicken bones for stock and throw in the onion and carrot ends we'd been saving, too. Then Shimi trims the sushi-quality tuna that arrived as one ten-pound hunk into eight-inch-long, two-inch-thick logs that will be seared tomorrow. He holds the first eight-inch log near his crotch for all to see.

"Most women find me uncomfortable," he giggles.

"I find you uncomfortable," I yell.

Kitchen folks talk about three things: sex, food, and bowel movements. It does not necessarily occur in this order, but it always occurs. Other subjects are subcategories of these three: comparing food items to genitalia, what other chefs are doing that we hate, and fart jokes.

In eight hours, we finish the day's prep. The chicken is marinating in fresh rosemary and garlic. The fish is cleaned. Twenty pounds of shrimp are peeled and deveined. Four legs of lamb are cut into kebab-size pieces and are marinating in toasted coriander, black pepper, olive oil, and fresh lemon juice. The sauces are done: one quart cilantro chutney dipping sauce, three quarts balsamic vinaigrette poured into squeeze bottles, six quarts apricot mustard glaze for chicken, one quart Creole cocktail sauce for tomorrow's grilled shrimp, one squirt bottle of wasabi aioli for the seared tuna, six quarts sherry and sage lentil salad dressing, four quarts of roasted red pepper coulis for salmon.

It's a light day.

Saturday morning begins as all my prewedding mornings do, with a huge cup of lethally strong coffee and a banana chaser. I take out the menu and make my food and equipment packing list.

My packing list would make NASA jealous: tuna, wasabi, ginger, chives, spatula, chef jackets, tongs, knife, thermometer, bamboo skewers, aprons, hot pads, spoons, pastry bag, three birthday candles for bride's flower girl, Rolaids for father of groom, Ziplocs to make doggie bags for bride's mom.

I pick up coffee for the crew and head over the bridge. Once in the kitchen, Shimi and Niko are in full crank mode.

Shimi is rotating ten sheet pans of chicken so they cook evenly. The dishwasher is julienning peppers. Niko is tossing the baby carrots in olive oil, salt, and pepper, then laying them on sheet pans to roast. The potatoes are already trayed up and waiting their turn.

To an outsider, we must look like a movie on fast-forward, but to us it's the usual prewedding motion. As long as we don't sit down or eat anything heavy, we can maintain this pace for up to ten hours.

In three hours, the preparty prep is done.

My Ecuadoran driver has arrived with the refrigerated van and is loading up the lugs, humming his usual song, which no one has heard of, not even the dishwasher.

We put our dirty gigantic chef jackets in the laundry bag and change into clean gigantic chef jackets.

Then we all cram into the van like the Beverly Hillbillies and head to the party.

We unload into the freight elevator at the party location, a Soho-style loft in Queens. The Ecuadoran elevator man politely helps us unload, using gentle encouragement: "Hurry the fuck up! I got things to do!"

In the top-floor party room, I find Margot, my maître d'. She has that look on her face that can only be read as, "Someone is pissing me off, big time!"

The bride's florist has decided to hang curtains in a way that blocks heat from circulating around the room, so the kitchen feels like Miami and the ceremony area feels like Siberia. The florist has also placed votive candles directly under her flower arrangements, and at least one arrangement has already caught fire.

In the kitchen, Niko and Shimi work on getting all the perishables organized and in the fridge. I take over setting up the eight-foot cheese table, and our other Ecuadoran dishwasher (what can I say, I'm the Ecuadoran employment agency) scrubs down the worktables.

The country-style cheese table is set for 175 guests with enough food on it to feed 300. The centerpiece is two dozen tricolor baguettes shooting into the air. Niko gets the hot hors d'oeuvres—400 vegetable dumplings, 350 potato latkes, 375 lamb kebabs, 400 vegetable samosas— trayed up on sheet pans for fast heating. Shimi slices the sesame-crusted seared tuna onto crispy wonton triangles, places a smidgen of pickled ginger in the corner of each, then drizzles a *Z* in wasabi aioli across the top. The guests, as always, arrive a half hour early.

For the next hour, we crank out hors d'oeuvres. Ira, the waiter in charge of letting us know what everyone in the entire room is saying and doing, comes in to report the essentials: how many of the guests are gay, how many are fat, who is a pig, what they think of the food, and what he thinks of the bride's outfit.

"Thanks Ira . . . Now shut up," I answer.

Six wedding guests station themselves at the exit to the kitchen and refuse to let the waiters get past them until after they've grabbed handfuls of everything on the trays.

"Um, we do have to get to the other guests," one of the waiters says politely.

"More shrimp!" they scream.

The waiters resort to battle mode. One waiter goes in front to make way, and the other waiter, with his tray up high over his head, pushes past the rude people and gets to the other guests.

We have thirty minutes to get ready for dinner.

I lay sides of pepper-roasted salmon on the fish tray. I zigzag red pepper coulis over the fish Jackson Pollock–style, then sprinkle thin-sliced scallions on top.

Shimi places the chicken, now steaming hot and glazed in caramelized apricot, on two large antique pewter trays. He spills extra apricot sauce on top and sprinkles each generously with chives. The corners of the trays are garnished with whole hands of fresh ginger. We toss the roasted root vegetables, fennel, golden beet, potato, and carrots, together and top with fresh chopped parsley, then serve in large wooden bowls. I build a couscous mountain.

This entails taking a Moroccan brass tray about the size of a Manhattan studio apartment, piling it with couscous until I have something out of *Close Encounters of the Third Kind*, then sprinkling the whole thing with white raisins, almonds, cashews, apricots, figs, and parsley.

It takes two of our butchest waiters to bring it out.

In twenty-nine minutes, we are ready. Just in time for a stampede worthy of any Western.

There aren't too many hitches in the dinner hour. A few old ladies refuse to get up, despite the fact that this is a buffet, and need to have their meals brought to them. A few more flower arrangements threaten to burst into flames. Nothing we can't handle.

Margot comes in for refills on baby lettuce salad and salmon. "That florist was trying to boss me around. Can you imagine? I said, 'Listen, honey, I've been running these weddings for twelve years. How long have you been around?'"

"You go, girl," I say, knowing exactly what happens to the silly mortals who try to boss Margot around.

After we have fed all the guests at least once, and some of them three times, the buffet is broken down. The florist, who is now noticeably drunk, comes into the kitchen to eat from the staff meal I've put out for the waiters. She is halfway through her meal before I notice she isn't using silverware.

"Here's a fork," I offer.

"Thanks."

Ira comes into the kitchen to eat. "Did you see that one who tried to eat the garnish? I was like, 'Lady, that's a flower.'"

I line up twelve assorted trays and bowls and mismatched antique mirrors on the back table. Niko begins making cookie and pastry displays for the dessert buffet. On one large antique mirror, he builds a giant *S* in brownie bites, then spills macaroons, shortbread cookies, mini chocolate chip cookies, baby pecan pies, coconut rum balls, rugelach, and fresh strawberries all around it, plopping orchids in the corners.

"Nice," I say, patting him on the back.

We hear the bandleader announce that it's time to cut the cake, even though it isn't nearly time to cut the cake. We hurriedly clear off our worktable and put cutting boards and knives on the table, as well as cake plates.

The cake the bride had insisted on buying from a cheap bakery comes in. We take the top layer off to save for the bride and groom, and Shimi and Niko start slicing the rest. Slicing it, thanks to a thick, greasy, somewhat-melted buttercream icing, is a gooey mess and it is (natch) exactly at this moment that the party location runs out of hot water.

Nothing short of gasoline will get melted buttercream off our fingers.

The 175 wedding guests, who have eaten food for 250, devour the baby pastry and cookie displays and still have plenty of room for cake.

Ira comes in the kitchen, "Did you see the guy who tried to eat the whole piece of ginger? I was like, 'Mista . . . I don't think you should be doing that.'"

In unison, we scream, "SHUT UP, IRA!"

We came, we saw, we fed the masses, and now there's a big-ass mess to haul back to the kitchen.

On the way out the door, I say goodnight to the elevator man. "Get the fuck out of here already!" he screams, giving me the finger.

**My two cents:** *The true art of wedding food is finding recipes that can't be ruined—foolproof food. Weddings never stay on schedule. If the guests are supposed to eat at nine, they may wind up chowing down at ten, or worse yet, they may demand dinner at 8:15 p.m. Sometimes they even walk in the door asking for supper.*

*Therefore, you need to invent recipes that can stand the heat of the chafing dish (the kryptonite of fine food), can be held in the oven for ten times longer than you expect, or can sit out at room temperature until your social security check arrives. Catering is a magnet for God's wacky sense of humor. You never know what She will throw at you.*

*The following recipes can stand up against anything short of an elephant or the uncle of the bride . . . often pretty much the same thing.*

## Herbie the Salmon

*Serves 6 to 10 people*

**INGREDIENTS**

**SALMON**

*1 whole salmon filet with no bones (about 3 lbs.)*
*Salt and fresh ground pepper*
*A few good drizzles olive oil*

**HERB CRUST**

*1 bunch or heaping handful each fresh parsley and*
*    cilantro, chopped*
*1 heaping plop garlic, minced*
*A few more good drizzles olive oil*

Start with a whole filet of salmon, meaning the entire side. Have your fish guy or gal scale and debone them for you, then check for bones. Season the salmon with salt and fresh ground pepper and brush on olive oil.

Lay the fish skin side down on baking sheets or what we in the biz call sheet pans.

Make an herb crust by throwing equal parts cleaned and chopped parsley and cilantro into the food processor. Then throw in a heaping plop of minced garlic and a few drizzles of olive oil to bring it around. If you don't have a food processor or blender, do this by hand and get prepared to work really hard. Don't say I didn't tell you.

Crust the top of the fish by spooning the herb mixture over it and rubbing it around until the salmon is evenly coated. It should look pretty and green like a picnic.

Bake at 400 degrees for about 20 minutes or until the salmon is cooked, which will vary depending on how large and thick the fish is and how well you like it cooked. I know it's blasphemy, but I like my fish cooked through. Season with salt and pepper, and you're done.

If you don't cook a whole filet, just individual portions, figure more like 10 to 15 minutes cooking time.

# Butternut Squash Soup Shots

*Serves 70 people*

One of my favorite passed hors d'oeuvres is soup shots. This one is killer for fall weddings. You can use this same recipe for pumpkin soup and carrot soup, too!

**INGREDIENTS**
*3 butternut squashes, peeled and cut up into chunks*
*2 cinnamon sticks*
*A few good plops brown sugar*
*3 heaping plops sweet butter*
*Salt and fresh ground white pepper*

**OPTIONAL**
*Reduced balsamic vinegar*
*Sliced chives*
*Crème fraîche*
*Ground cumin, coriander, curry, or nutmeg*
*Apple cider*

Peel and cut about 3 butternut squashes into chunks. I admit this takes some muscle, but it's worth it. Breathe, baby, breathe!

Submerge your cut squash in water just enough to cover, and float two cinnamon sticks and a few good plops of brown sugar right in the water. Bring to a boil, then lower to a medium roll and cook till soft.

Drain and puree your hot squash with the cooking liquid, hold the cinnamon sticks, and add a lot of sweet butter. Like 3 heaping plops.

Season with salt and white pepper, and add enough cooking water to make things soupy but thick, like a good gravy. Then you can use a funnel or whatever contraption you prefer and pour into shot glasses.

Sometimes I garnish this with a drizzle of reduced balsamic vinegar, sometimes some sliced chives, sometimes a little dollop of crème fraîche, but usually I just keep as is. It's so darn good!

To jazz things up, I add a pinch of cumin, coriander, or curry, sometimes nutmeg. Sometimes I add apple cider to the soup, but, like I said, it's pretty darn good as is!

# I Did It All for ~~Love~~ Chicken

*Serves 6 people*

This is really good, so cook at least 6 breasts, even if you're only having dinner for 2. It's even better as a leftover.

**INGREDIENTS**
*2 shots olive oil*
*A few drizzles fresh lemon juice*
*2 pinches fresh oregano, chopped*
*1 plop garlic, minced*
*6 or more boneless chicken breasts*
*1 good pinch salt and fresh ground pepper*

Mix a couple shots of olive oil with a couple drizzles of fresh lemon juice, a couple pinches of fresh chopped oregano, a plop of minced garlic, and a good pinch of fresh ground pepper. Drop in boneless chicken breasts and marinate overnight or at least for a couple hours.

To cook, pan sear your chicklets on both sides in a hot skillet till well browned, then throw in the oven for 10 or 15 minutes till done. Add salt and pepper to taste. Serve topped with Turkish Salad.

## Turkish Salad

*Serves the 6 eating the I Did It All for ~~Love~~ Chicken*

### INGREDIENTS
*1 drizzle red wine vinegar*
*1 shot olive oil*
*Salt and fresh ground pepper*
*1 plop fresh parsley, chopped*
*3 ripe tomatoes, diced*
*2 handfuls red bell pepper, diced*
*1 handful cucumber, diced*
*½ red onion, diced*

### OPTIONAL
*Fresh mint*

Make a dressing out of good red wine vinegar and about 1½ times as much of extra virgin olive oil. Whisk up your dressing, then add in some salt and pepper.

Mix up your fresh chopped parsley, ripe tomatoes, bell peppers, cucumber, red onion, and your dressing. You can adjust the seasoning to your liking. Some folks add fresh mint, too.

# Vagina Power

I am rarely called upon to cater "normal" events. I suppose that has something to do with the name I chose for my company. Nobody asks a company called the Raging Skillet to provide tea sandwiches and scones. That is, of course, unless those tea sandwiches are peanut butter and bacon and the scones are served with habañero chutney.

One day, I got a call from a woman named Sally Fisher. She was Eve Ensler's pal and producer, and she wanted me to cater a party on Valentine's Day. Turns out, it was the hottest ticket in town: twenty female celebs, including Glenn Close, Rosie Perez, Whoopi Goldberg, Barbara Walters, Gloria Steinem, Marisa Tomei, Lily Tomlin, Hazelle Goodman, Calista Flockhart, and Susan Sarandon, would perform excerpts from Eve's hit off-Broadway show, *The Vagina Monologues*. An actress, performance artist, activist, and global icon, Eve created the show by asking hundreds of women one question: "If your vagina could talk, what would it say?" This performance would also mark the launch of V-Day, the organization Eve founded to stop violence against women worldwide.

Before we got off the phone, Sally said, rather demurely in her raspy voice, "We'd like all the food served to be, shall we say, anatomically correct!" I knew then that life as I knew it was about to get so much more delicious.

It took some doing, but as I wove layer over layer of sun-dried fruit—apricots, apple slices, pineapple rings, and papaya spears—along a four-foot oval, it began to resemble my vision: a giant, edible vagina. When it was all but done, I placed one strategic sun-dried cranberry on the money spot and asked two of my strongest waiters to help me carry it to the green room at the Hammerstein Ballroom.

The stars, wearing red for the occasion, hovered around my fruit homage backstage. Glenn Close, looking regal with her platinum hair cut very short, delicately reached in and took a bit of fruit from an outer layer. Hazelle Goodman, whose one-woman show had critics calling her "the next Whoopi Goldberg," showed off her muscular arms in a red tank top as she folded a slice of apricot into her mouth. Marisa Tomei, topping off her outfit with a red boa, admired my masterpiece and gave it a thumbs-up before taking a slice of apple.

Just then, Susan Sarandon swept in, breaking all the rules. In a brown leather jacket and dark brown silk blouse, she ran to the fruit-gina, rubbed her hands with glee, and popped the strategically placed sun-dried cranberry in her mouth, giggling with delight. As suddenly as she had appeared, she was gone. Her towering beau, Tim Robbins, grinned and said, "I think she liked that!"

"That's it!" I said to my laughing waiters. "Right here and now, this is my all-time-favorite catering moment! Susan Sarandon just ate my . . . " Well, you get the point.

It was a sold-out crowd of 2,500 with more waiting on the street hoping to get in. The all-star cast brought down the house, and those of us backstage were breathless and spent after the final monologue, in which Eve herself performed an orgasm that threatened to lift the roof.

"That's gonna be a tough act to follow," Marisa Tomei whispered.

"I'm gonna follow it with a sea of vaginas," I whispered back.

I'd built a giant display with a store mannequin that I covered completely in rose petals. From the rose torso spilled sliced persimmons, sun-dried pear slices, and a bounty of any kind of fruit that looked fertile when sliced. Over this, I spilled waterfalls of cheeses cut into triangles and ovals. The "rose lady" was the center of an exploding fountain of abundance.

My chefs and I also prepared themed hors d'oeuvres, including tuna tartare arranged along oval sliced cucumbers with a puff of black seaweed on the top, chili-dusted smoked salmon swirled into vaginal roses and placed on triangle crisps of naan topped with sweet onion chutney, and crispy fried plantain chips with paper-thin Korean Barbecued Beef ribboned down their center and a well-placed drizzle of red miso.

The celebs were ready to unwind.

Rosie Perez, who had been so frightened backstage that her teeth were chattering, had performed several different women talking about their first period.

"Thank gawd that's ovah!" she screamed in her Puerto-Rican-by-way-of-Brooklyn accent, popping half an outer labia's worth of apricots into her mouth.

Rosie, who had barely eaten all day due to nerves, parted the curtain and charged into my kitchen.

"Oh, I just want to try a little of this and that," she announced, as she grazed her way through all of my concoctions. "I'm sorry . . . but you know . . . I was too freaked out to eat, and now I'm starrrrrrrrrving," she chattered away, stuffing artichoke hearts and dumplings into her mouth. She was so cute I let her stay, though as a rule, I don't like civilians in my kitchen.

Shimi immediately began a spot-on Rosie Perez imitation.

"Ummm this is so good 'cause it's really good, you know?" he squealed, making her laugh so hard she snorted.

Rosie screamed in near ecstasy when she was the first guest to see our finale, one thousand pairs of lips made of red chocolate.

"Oh God, this is so wonderful, I mean, this is delicious, I mean, where I'm from we don't have this. I mean, what is this?" she shouted in delirium, swallowing a slice of papaya that looked like a Georgia O'Keeffe painting, then chasing it with a pair of chocolate lips and bundling two more with a half-dozen dumplings into a napkin. "You know, f' latah . . . ," she said, blowing kisses on her way out of the kitchen.

By the time I joined the after-party, most of the six hundred VIPs had left, but the hundred or so who were still there began to clap. Sally ran over and hugged me, "Thank you for making the V-Day launch simply spectacular! Your vaginas were delicious!"

Eve bowed her head from across the room, and I curtsied.

"I think you're going to be very busy," Sally added. "People were asking for your number all night."

She was right. A year after the V-Day party, *New York* magazine included me in its feature "Party Like It's 1999" as its pick for one of New York's best caterers, and my phone started ringing like mad. Zagat anointed me "the wildest thing this side of the Mason-Dixon Line." I appeared on the Food Network's *Cooking Live* show. I even got to feed the president! Clinton, that is. Love that man.

To this day, when I am asked what my favorite catering moment is, I think back to Valentine's Day 1998, the highlight of my entire catering career, and answer, "Vagina power!"

# Tuna Tartare

*Serves 4 to 6 people*

I have made tuna tartare loads of different ways, but I'm partial to going Asian.

**INGREDIENTS**

*1 lb. tuna, sushi quality*
*1 drizzle tamari*
*1 drizzle sesame oil*
*1 little drizzle vegetable oil*
*1 smidgen ground fresh ginger*
*1 handful white sesame seeds*
*1 cucumber or daikon, cut into ¼-inch circle slices*

Start with sushi-quality tuna 'cause you are eating this raw, after all. One pound will do ya. Cube up your tuna into the smallest dice you can manage. If there are any dark parts to the slab, cut it out, and feed it to the cat.

Make a dressing out of your tamari, sesame oil, vegetable oil, and fresh ginger.

Meanwhile, toast a handful of white sesame seeds in a hot pan until they are a bit scorched.

About 10 minutes to a half hour before you are ready to serve, toss your tuna and dressing together. Spoon a nice amount on a slice of cucumber, or a slice of peeled

daikon, and garnish with the toasted sesame seeds.
I made mine look like vaginas, but you don't have to.
Gorgeous fresh tuna is sexy enough.

# Korean Barbecued Beef

*Serves 2 for dinner or 6 as an hors d'oeuvre*

## INGREDIENTS

*1 lb. flank steak cleaned of extra fat*
*and silver skin*
*2 drizzles sesame oil*
*2 drizzles soy sauce*
*1 drizzle rice wine vinegar*
*1 handful scallion, sliced*
*1 plop garlic, minced*
*1 plop Chinese chili paste*
*A few slices fresh ginger*

For the Jewish Korean marinade, mix 2 drizzles of sesame oil, 2 drizzles of soy sauce, 1 drizzle of rice wine vinegar, a handful of sliced scallions, a plop of fresh minced garlic, a plop of Chinese chili paste (almost any kind), and a few large slices of fresh ginger. Marinate your flank steak in a bowl with your marinade overnight.

Grill your flank steak about 5 minutes per side and let cool. It should be super rare.

Slice across the grain into strips as thin as you can and ribbon them onto a skewer or into a lettuce cup. Serve with the Korean Drizzle. Ribbon onto toasted plantain chips with red miso paste for a more authentic V-Day presentation.

# Korean Drizzle

*Serve with Korean Barbecued Beef*

### INGREDIENTS
*2 red bell peppers, roasted and peeled*
*1 heaping plop miso paste*
*1 good drizzle soy sauce or tamari*

The sauce is made by pureeing a handful of roasted
and peeled red bell peppers mixed with a heaping plop
of miso paste and a good drizzle of soy sauce or tamari.
Drizzle the sauce generously over your beef, and top
with sliced scallions.

# Rabbis and Mozzarella

Twenty years after being abandoned in Crown Heights, I was dragged back to my former home by my brother, who had embraced all things Jewish. I was thirty-six years old and far too busy running my company to traipse around Hasidic-ville, but there is simply no saying no to my family. Besides, there was something about the new millennium that made me want to go back to my old home/prison.

The first thing my brother said after landing at JFK Airport—besides saying his kids needed a bathroom, his wife was nauseated, and that he was dying for some kosher fried mozzarella—was that he wanted to visit 770.

I have to say I was shocked. Why would *anyone* who lived in Beverly Hills want to visit 770, the rustic old synagogue in Crown Heights? Maybe all the color in Beverly Hills made him long for Brooklyn browns—brownstones, brown brick, and brown paper bags thrown on the ground.

Then again, I never understood why Matt moved to

California. How could anyone with the option to live in New York City move to LA?

Anyway, back to 770, the big draw was the rebbe, of course—the man I'd admired as a teen, despite myself. Rebbe Schneerson had passed away years ago, and a lot of his followers were breaking rank with other Jews because they considered him to be the Messiah.

I kinda thought the rebbe would have liked the idolization about as much as peace-loving Jesus would have liked the Crusades. I hadn't left Crown Heights with a high regard for fanaticism.

My brother more than wanted to visit the rebbe's shul; he had to see it. He had always hungered for anything intensely Jewish, whether it was those kosher mozzarella sticks or, now, the shul.

I figured it was something about never fitting in when he was a kid. Being Jewish gave him the group affinity he'd always craved. It culminated in the epiphany that he and his Israeli wife, Dahlia, had six years earlier, after which they'd decided to ditch their fast-food lifestyle and become ultra-Orthodox.

So we went to 770. Matt rented a sedan so we could cruise Eastern Parkway in style.

Matt had another reason beyond the Judaic gravitational pull for wanting to visit the Lubavitch section of Crown Heights. He wanted to see where I'd disappeared to during those long, strange years after I moved out of the house and didn't call, write, or express any of the signs of overwhelming guilt demanded by our mother.

He was dragging me back to the place I had spent all my energy and money trying to escape. All the way there, I was thinking what I've thought since I was two years old: surely, I am adopted.

We parked on a side street, and Matthew led the kids along, as his wife videotaped every storefront on the avenue. When we got to the corner, the old industrial shell of the shul shot up before us. Matthew screamed for his wife: "Quick! Dahlia, it's 770!"

She videotaped Matt touching the brick wall, Matt walking up the stairs, her little girls, Francis and Harriet, touching the walls, Francis and Harriet walking up the stairs. She videotaped me rolling my eyes, me trying not to go up the stairs, me kicking at her when she tried to push me up the stairs, me waving and winking at a horrified young Hasid man who was staring at my not-so-kosher tattoo.

Inside the shul, Matthew went down to the open, airy room with the pumped-in air-conditioning to pray with the men, while Dahlia let the girls drag their tattooed aunt to the claustrophobic, poorly ventilated women's section upstairs. All was just as I'd remembered it: a scattering of siddur prayer books and those painful wooden benches, thick with layers of dull brown paint.

Peering down onto the main floor, I could see Matthew praying while a few dozen rabbis-to-be argued over semantics and whatever. He was thrilled to be there and seemed to be praying as much to be seen by these men as to be heard by the Almighty.

Dahlia watched her husband with pride. After a few minutes, I opted to wait outside where they keep this stuff called air.

As much as 770 was the same, it was newly quiet, especially for the High Holidays. Missing were the thousands of visitors who used to pour onto the streets. I guessed the rebbe's death had changed that.

A few tour buses disgorged loads of bewigged women in long skirts over jogging suits at all the pertinent rebbe stops. His former office. His former home. At each place, you could hear the excited tour guide scream into her microphone, "And this was actually where the rebbe lived . . . and . . . [gasp] . . . slept!"

I wondered if they had the whole shebang on the tour. "This is where the rebbe once used the bathroom. Over here, he had a sandwich. At this corner, he hailed a cab."

We passed all the places I remembered from my teen years—the dairy luncheonette, the Puerto Rican bodega with Hector and the gang, hairy-chested men wearing lots of gold chains, Weinstein's Hardware, and a multitude of Judaica gift shops.

The shop windows were filled with rebbe keepsakes: rebbe T-shirts, key chains, postcards, photo albums. Crown Heights had turned into Rebbe Graceland.

While Dahlia checked out the key chains, Matthew began his mezuzah interrogation. He was on a mission to find a scroll for the mezuzah on my doorjamb that would be so holy, so pure that it would vaporize nonkosher Chinese delivery before it could enter my apartment.

It was my own fault; I'd asked him to help me find a scroll. After more than three decades, he was so thrilled to finally have me ask for his help that he turned it into a full-scale mission.

"This doesn't feel right," he said to Dahlia, fingering a tiny scroll. "Let's keep looking."

In high-tech full color, a banner bearing the rebbe's image stretched across Kingston Avenue. It announced, "Welcome Moshiach!"

A flag waved the words, "Moshiach is on the way. Be a part of it."

As if on cue, Matthew announced, "Let's eat!" and led us along Kingston Avenue in search of kosher mozzarella sticks.

We found the kosher pizza joint, which now sported a bright neon sign reading "Kingston Pizza." The owners must have sold out to restaurateurs with a flair for technology. Inside felt more like a Wendy's than a Jewish pizza parlor. Full-color fluorescent signboards offered tahini, baba ghanoush, falafel, and pizza. I stuck with the safe: falafel and iced tea.

Matthew ordered an array of dishes: baked ziti, French fries, pizza, falafel, fried fish, Israeli salad, and, of course, fried mozzarella.

It was a heartburn parade, and my brother was its grand marshal.

A group of yeshiva boys walked into the pizza joint. They looked at Matt with mild concern until they saw his yarmulke, then nodded with approval. As they passed our booth they saw me and got that look of consternation I'd seen many times in this neighborhood: "What's a bad girl like you doing in a place like this?"

In the old days, when I would bang up against that look, one of the locals would say, "Baal teshuvah," and everyone would laugh.

Baal teshuvah, the name given to Jews who are not brought up frum, excuses everything from apparent schizophrenia to earrings made out of coke spoons.

To amuse myself in the old days, I used to talk to myself loudly, and when one of the locals would give me a concerned look, I would smile and say, "Baal teshuvah." Hey, a girl's got to have a little fun.

We walked by my old flat on Kingston. Visions of my huge bachelorette pad nestled over the pharmacy danced in my head. The two-bedroom place for which we'd paid a whopping $250 a month was now a podiatrist's shop.

I remembered the parties with chairs made of milk crates and the overturned basket turned coffee table, the feasts I prepared for my mishmash of local pals. I remembered the faces, so intent on my every word, so clearly temporary despite all their pretenses of love and affection. Everything then was temporary. Even the plates were paper.

Fagee, my Parisian roommate, surfaced many years later at my bar on the top deck of the *Matthew Rousseau* with a doctor husband and a glass of chardonnay.

"Remember how wild we were?" she cooed.

"Yes," I answered, remembering, too, how poor we were, how bad the neighborhood was, and, deep inside, how wild we really weren't.

"This is where your Aunt Rossi used to live," Dahlia told the girls.

"That's right, kiddies. I once blessed this place with my bubbling personality."

"Woooowwwwww!" they screamed, and danced in front of the two-story building.

At the end of Kingston, Matthew found a shop owned by the uncle of the nephew of a friend of his friend in Los Angeles and decided this would be the place pious enough to have the right mezuzah scrolls for his sister.

While I fingered through a book of recipes for dishes like "Mock Chopped Liver"—yum—Matthew haggled.

"Give me a good price," my brother told the old man. "I've come all the way from California."

Seventy-five dollars and forty minutes later, I had a bag with two mezuzah scrolls guaranteed to keep treif from my doorstep, and we were back in the silver town car on Eastern Parkway pointed toward Manhattan.

Ahhhh, Manhattan. Just knowing we were heading toward that isle of sanity sent a soothing calm through me.

"Your aunt met the rebbe," Dahlia said to the girls.

"Reallyyyyy?" they squeaked excitedly.

"Yep. One time he gave me a shot of wine, and the other time he gave me a piece of bread."

"Ooooooooohhh," the girls squealed.

"Did he ever give you . . . a mozzarella stick?"

They are, after all, my brother's children.

# Super, Super Fast and Zingy Falafel

*Serves 4 to 6 people*

Well kids . . . following that journey into Kvetchland, here are some of my brother's favorite noshes.

**INGREDIENTS**

*2 coffee cups dry chickpeas, soaked in water overnight*
*A few plops garlic, minced*
*1 handful onion, minced*
*1 pinch ground cumin*
*1 pinch ground coriander*
*1 handful fresh parsley, chopped*
*1 handful fresh cilantro, chopped*
*1 drizzle fresh lemon juice*
*1 pinch baking soda*
*Salt and fresh ground pepper*

Puree 2 coffee cups of the soaked and drained chickpeas. I always buy chickpeas dry and soak them in water overnight before cooking.

Anyway . . . puree 2 coffee cups of the chickpeas, and toss in a few plops of minced garlic, a handful of onion, a pinch of cumin, a pinch of coriander, a handful of chopped parsley, a handful of chopped cilantro, and a little drizzle of lemon juice. Scrape your batter into a bowl and then mix in baking soda. Adjust to your liking with salt and pepper and leave batter in the fridge until you're ready to roll.

You can form patties out of this, sorta like little hamburgers. Or you can go with meatball shapes.

In a deep pot or skillet filled with about two to three inches of oil, fry on medium heat until crispy and golden.

I like to serve this in a pita with Turkish Salad, Tahini Dressing, and a bit of hot sauce. It's killer!

## Tahini Dressing

*Serve with Super, Super Fast and Zingy Falafel*

**INGREDIENTS**
*3 plops tahini*
*1 drizzle fresh lemon juice*
*2 drizzles cold water*
*1 pinch garlic, minced*
*1 pinch salt*

Mix 3 plops of tahini with lemon juice, water, and a pinch of fresh garlic. Salt to taste.

## Mozzarella Sticks

*Serves 6 normal people or 3 of my relatives*

### INGREDIENTS

*1 lb. mozzarella, cut into finger-size shapes*
*2 eggs*
*1 shot water*
*1 coffee cup bread crumbs*
*1 coffee cup flour*
*Salt and fresh ground pepper*
*Garlic powder*
*Vegetable oil*

Cut mozzarella into fingers. For this you will want the packaged mozzarella, not the fresh kind that's too watery and too good for cheap eats like mozzarella sticks.

Mix 2 eggs with a shot of water. Fill one bowl with bread crumbs and one bowl with flour. Season one of them well with salt, pepper, and garlic powder . . . doesn't matter which one.

Now get some vegetable oil super hot in a deep pot or saucepan or wok.

Dip your mozzarella in the flour, then the egg, then the bread crumbs. At this point you can fry as is but for killer results, go back to dip in the egg and bread crumbs again. The double dipping makes a huge difference.

# Days of Awe

A lot of folks I meet seem to be under the delusion that being a caterer is like a constant Hollywood-red-carpet way to make a living. "Oh, you must meet so many famous people!" they exclaim.

"Uh-huh," I reply, thinking of the bused tray that came back into the kitchen with a half-bitten crostini, lipstick on the eaten part. "Cher ate that!" screamed one of my waiters.

Behind the scenes, catering is anything but a posh experience. After days of marinating hundreds of pounds of meat and simmering vats of sauce, it's then the main event: high adrenaline, high stress, in the trenches, get it done—deliciously and gorgeously—on time for two hundred impatient and hungry guests, and don't forget to sprinkle some chives on its way out of the kitchen.

It's not easy, but it's also anything but boring.

I took the adrenaline rush for granted. Then 9/11 happened, and I realized that the crazy way we caterers make a living can actually make us pretty darn good to have around when the world feels like it's coming apart.

On September 16, 2001, after spending every day since the eleventh walking up and down the West Side Highway trying to volunteer but finding no one who would take me, a woman whose wedding I was supposed to cater called to tell me it was canceled because the city had turned her party space, Seamen's Church Institute, from a maritime museum and party space into a home for hundreds of rescue workers. There was no electricity, no plumbing, and no running water, and they were trying to feed, clothe, and give counsel to anyone who could get to them.

By the time I showed up at Seamen's, Billy and Dominic were already there unloading trucks of supplies. Billy and Dominic are the security guards at the Institute, sweet men whom I've gotten to be pals with over many years of catering events there. They were both wide eyed and pale. Dominic's head was wrapped in a flag, and he hadn't shaved in days.

"We were trapped in the tunnel when it happened," Billy said. "I had to walk out and leave Dominic. He told me just go, go."

The best man from Dominic's wedding was among the missing. "There's no way. He was on the seventy-sixth floor!" Dominic said. "I can't think about it . . . Just keep moving! I've been here since day one, haven't been home in a week."

It didn't take much to get me on board. "She's a chef," Dominic told the man in charge, who gave me a volunteer pass, a hard hat, and a ventilator and put me on a pickup truck headed to Ground Zero.

"She's going to St. Paul's!" someone said.

"Where's St. Paul's?" I asked the driver.

"Next door to the Millennium Hotel. They say it's stable."

We were led through police barricades and armed guards until the truck finally dropped us at the church.

The old brown church had a row of portable toilets to the right and a long stretch of tables to the left. The tables were covered with everything from hot dogs to thermoses filled with coffee. There were boxes of doughnuts, eye solution, Band-Aids, hundreds of apples, and thousands of bottles of Gatorade on ice. Dozens of firefighters, cops, and construction workers were in line to eat, and a small group of women were doing their best to keep up with the hot dog requests on two small backyard barbecue grills.

I added coals to the dying fires, threw on a few more packs of hot dogs, and looked for anything resembling a pair of tongs.

St. Paul's dates back to 1762. George Washington prayed there, and amid the devastation it stood, covered in dust and dirt but unharmed. Each step leading into the chapel held a different box of clothing or supplies: socks, flannel shirts, work gloves, secondhand hard hats. Inside on some of the wooden pews, police officers sat collecting their thoughts. Soldiers napped in the last few rows.

I set up my grills in front of the church's cemetery. Two-hundred-year-old tombstones, so old their inscriptions had long since eroded, poked out from piles of burned and charred papers from the World Trade Center. I looked at one piece of paper, a bit of banking business of some kind, a cover letter from a fax.

"Have you been given the drill yet?" a woman asked me. She was stuffing hot dogs into buns.

"No."

"If you hear the alarm, you've got to run around and out of the gate. Then run as fast as you can, that way toward the seaport."

"Okay," I said.

On my second day grilling for the workers, I was taken on a cold drink run to the Hole. I went with one of the guys, pushing a wheelbarrow filled with ice and Gatorade. The Hole was the deep collapsed area at Ground Zero, adjacent to the Pile, where the debris was stacked more than seven stories high.

Soldiers guarding the Hole let us by, allowing us to go to the tent set up less than one hundred feet from the remains of the second tower. Smoke and steam rose from the wreckage as firefighters on their fresh-air breaks sat motionless a few feet away. Nothing I'd seen on the news had prepared me for this. Sharp, burned bits of metal jutted up fifty or one hundred feet—I have no idea how high. I had to crane my neck to find their tops. Over my head were these shards of bent, broken metal. In the background was total destruction.

*Me and two heroes of St. Paul's Church at Ground Zero (2001).*

"I'll take one of those!" a silver-haired firefighter said, and I handed him a Gatorade.

"Where you from?" he asked.

"I live here," I said.

He took off his helmet and ran his fingers along his scalp. "I'm sorry for what they did to your city. We just flew in from California to help out."

I said thanks and felt dizzy from the weight of what I could see in my peripheral vision.

The tent was full of firefighters, and they cheered when we poured ice into their cooler of warm sodas and energy drinks. We handed around the cold Gatorades.

"I haven't had something cold to drink since 6:00 a.m.," one of the guys said. It was sometime after noon.

Later that day, Seamen's delivered two hunks of steel they'd welded into grills. Four-foot-long pits filled with charcoal sent up smoke and fire so intense I had to throw down a burger, then jump back. The legs were too tall, requiring Hector, the tallest griller among us, to stand on milk crates just to flip the burgers. I moved to the back-yard grills and tried to keep up.

When shifts changed, fifty rescue workers at a time showed up hungry for burgers. They settled for hot dogs when we ran out. Someone said we fed a thousand people on my second day.

"You guys are the best," said a carpenter from Queens.

"No. You're the hero," I said.

"Nah. We're all in this together. It's you guys feeding us and the people who run up with eye wash the second you rub your eyes and the people cheering you on as you drive in. That's the reason I can do what I do, because you all do what you do."

"Thank you," I said.

"Do you know how many times I've heard that since I've been out here? I can't even count them." He walked away shaking his head.

There was an air about Ground Zero that was not sadness so much as something like love. No one looked as though they had slept.

Steve, an out-of-work actor, had been there for a week. He threw foil-wrapped hot dogs directly into the Hole as fast as the men working below could catch them.

"More! More! I need at least a hundred hot dogs," Steve said. He was wired and pushy, but none of us took it to heart.

Scott supervised the many drugstore and clothing donations. He slept on a blanket on the floor of the church for a week.

"Are you with the church?" I asked.

"Nah, I just found my way here."

A pastor from another church came once to deliver ice and stayed for a week. His job was simple. He ran to Costco six times a day and bought all the burgers and dogs he could carry, then drove them back to Ground Zero.

Things changed on my third day. There had been no official statement, but everyone knew the rescue mission had become a cleanup mission. The pace of the workers slowed. There were no more news crews and no urgency in the air. People started to break down.

The dogs sent out to sniff for survivors had become

depressed. The crews took turns hiding so the shepherds and labs could find them. When the dog sniffed out the guy who was hiding, they received hearty praise and hugs.

I went on a relief run to the Hole and handed out packets of trail mix to the crews. They loved the chance to eat something healthy and took handfuls of the packets. A sign on a nearby dumpster read, "Airplane parts, FBI."

The men had a look on their faces that read, "It's over."

The Board of Health sent inspectors to make sure we wore plastic gloves. They asked us to wrap the apples in foil and cover the grills. The dust was a health hazard, they said.

"We're pretty sanitary over here," I said. "Are you worried we might be creating a health problem?"

"More like we're worried about your health," the inspector said.

One of the girls said, "They think the bodies might be creating a biohazard."

We also were told that they would shut us down soon.

"These guys are going to be down here for months," the inspector said. "We want to come up with a long-term way to deal with this, working with the local restaurants that have been closed."

The inspectors told us not to use the huge steel grills, as they have no covers, so we added a third backyard barbecue grill, and I ran back and forth, turning hot dogs and replacing the covers on each of the grills.

A truckload of replacement volunteers arrived to give us a break, but no one wanted to go.

"I think tomorrow might be the last day they let us do

this," Scott said, instructing the new crew on how to sort clothes and supplies. "I'll be here for as long as they'll let me stay."

I stayed until my eyes were blurry from smoke, then caught a pickup truck back to the seaport. Crowds of people took snapshots of us as we drove past, this motley crew in the bed of a truck with an American flag flying off a makeshift flagpole.

On my last day at Ground Zero, I skipped Rosh Hashanah services and got out to the site early, but I was delivering food to a gloomy crew. The Board of Health had shut down our grills and any food production. We were allowed to dole out only precooked burgers and sandwiches.

The trucks from Seamen's Church brought more than a thousand peanut butter and jelly sandwiches. None of the rescue workers were interested in peanut butter and jelly.

"No more burgers," a cop said. His hands were raw, beaten. He said he'd been digging out nothing but body parts all day.

"They just want us to pack up," said Roger, the volunteer who seemed the most like our leader. He wore a hard hat with an American flag taped to it.

I stepped into the church in search of serving utensils and found a dozen rescue workers sitting in the pews, most of them with tears in their eyes.

I took my last walk to Ground Zero. I delivered a bag of a hundred peanut butter and jelly sandwiches to the guards at the Pile. We were no longer allowed in to give them directly to the workers ourselves.

Back at the long row of donation tables set in front of the burned-out shell of Five World Trade Center, Brian, one of the guys who works for my catering company, sorted through boxes of underwear and T-shirts. He was organizing things to be sent elsewhere, perhaps to the Salvation Army.

As we commiserated on how this was a strange place to spend Rosh Hashanah, an amazing thing happened.

An army soldier with a long white beard stacked several plastic crates one on top of the other and placed a plastic shelf used to transport bread on top of the crates, forming a table. He covered the table with a blue velvet cloth, on which was embroidered a Star of David.

Then he set down a prayer book for the Days of Awe and a shofar.

As he began to recite the prayers, a group of Jewish soldiers gathered around him. Brian, some Jewish volunteers, and I heard the prayers and joined in.

Then, in front of the worst vision of death and ruin any of us will probably ever see, he blew the shofar. The sweet-sour, mournful sound of the ram's horn pierced the air and resonated into the distance.

The women began to cry. We kissed each other. "La Shanah Tovah!" we said, holding each other. We were all strangers. We probably would never see each other again, but we kissed and hugged like family.

The soldier with the shofar wore a tallis made in camouflage material. "Thank you so much," I said to him.

"Ah, it's nothing," he said, laughing and taking my hand in his. "This is the Army. I do this all the time."

## Peace Stew

*Serves all of humankind*

Mix one part love, one part compassion, one part hope, and one part forgiveness.

Hope for a better tomorrow.

# Niko the Invincible

Over the years, I have had chefs who were like family to me. But none of them quite so much as Niko, who morphed into a blend of a brother, son, and wife to me, though we had what appeared to be an unpromising start.

In the midst of my busy season, my pal Carolyn sent me a new recruit and told me that not only did he have more than twenty years of experience but he was also, lord help me, European. I assumed, naturally, that he would have the attitude of the king of England. And if there's gonna be a monarch in my kitchen, it's gonna be me. That's the benefit of being the boss.

My apprehension was not without due cause. In the catering biz, there are certain things cooks don't like to do after they've become chefs. One of the great downsides to this business is that you can always find a chef but never a cook, and, in reality, what you really want if you own your own business is a chef who can cook.

Don't get me started on the cook/chef thing because there are times when great chefs call themselves cooks, and, more often, there are times when lousy cooks call themselves chefs. In catering, the difference between the two comes down to about five bucks an hour. Cooks clearly less, chefs clearly more.

So as I said, there are certain things a cook will do and a chef will not, such as wash a dish or two if the dishwasher is in the bathroom or perhaps making drug deals on his cell phone. Don't ask.

A chef will not arrange bread baskets. This is "waiter's work." Likewise, a chef will not make butter plates. This is "waiter's or cook's work."

So when Carolyn sent over Chef Europe, whose name, Niko, sounded almost as pompous as I expected him to be, to join me as I was setting up for a wedding of 190, I was concerned.

"Helloo. I am Niko . . . You are . . . Rossi?" he asked, stepping into the kitchen dressed in immaculate chef whites that made mine look yellow.

"Yes . . . ," I said, shaking his hand. Then he said the most surprising thing.

"How may I help you?"

"Well," I said, suddenly feeling sheepish. "There are nineteen tables, and they all need butter plates."

"Ah," he said, smiling an eerie little smile that reminded me of cats after they've eaten.

He looked around the kitchen.

"What may I use as garnish?"

"Anything you want?"

"And may I make plates any way I want?"

"As long as they're pretty and hold enough butter for ten."

I went about the business of garnishing hors d'oeuvre trays, supervising the first course plating, and making sure the oven worked. On the periphery, I was vaguely aware of Niko cutting orchids.

After all the first-course plates were put out, it was time for the waiters to drop off the butter plates. It was only then that I saw what he had done: the butter plates were anything but, well, butter plates. They were skyscrapers of geometric butter shards, shooting up and out like an abstract painter's Fourth of July, giving birth as they exploded into a fluff of orchids, chives, and rosemary.

"Ohhhh!" the waiters gasped.

You can't imagine how hard it is to get a New York City cater waiter to gasp. In one attempt, I placed an entire shiitake mushroom in my nostril. It didn't work.

"They're beautiful!" the waiters cooed.

"Thank you. Now, what else may I do?" he asked, still smiling the fed-cat smile.

"Well, how 'bout carving the filet?"

"Certainly."

During the dinner, at which we served a gorgeous Asian-style salad with miso dressing followed by filet mignon in a tamari reduction, the waiters returned to the kitchen time and again to pass on the same message: "The guests are knocked out . . . by the butter plates."

I didn't know whether to laugh or cry. My gorgeous meal had been upstaged by a butter plate, but Niko had made his point.

I hired him immediately.

Without asking, he went over to the prep list taped to the walk-in, scrolled down, and picked the job everyone else was hoping would not drop in their lap: trimming one hundred pounds of filet mignon.

"I do this one . . . if it's okay with you."

"Suuuurrrrre."

"Suuuurrrrre," the rest of the team echoed, their fear of competition quickly assuaged by their knowledge that they would now see home before sundown.

From that point on, my former chef, Shimi, took to sitting in the bathroom when the prep list was posted. Once assured that Niko had begun the butchering, he would emerge saying, "That was a good one!" and go about an easier task.

It didn't take Niko long to introduce me to countless recipes. He showed me a new way to cook rice, a new way to cook orzo, a new way to marinate beef, a new way to do inventory, a new way to pack a party, and, well, a new way to live life.

"Sweetieeee," he said, as before all of his pronouncements, "do not get upset over some burned onions. Just throw them out and move on. There are better things to get upset about . . . just watch the news!"

Niko was also the first chef I'd met who shared my egalitarian view of the floor staff. Other chefs consider the waiters cattle, worthy only of being yelled at and herded off to fetch the chef a cocktail.

However, it is the waiter and not the chef who brings the food to the table. And my dears, no matter how much you work on a perfect duck breast in plum glaze, if the person bringing it to the table scowls and drops it like it's a stinking diaper, your guests will not be impressed.

While Shimi would bark out orders to the waiters—"Wipe your trays! Read the menu! Go away!"—Niko would quietly step outside and say to them, "Sweetie, would you mind cleaning your trays for us? We are so slammed. If you have questions let me know."

Not surprisingly, the service improved, and our jobs in the kitchen became easier.

Now, before you start to think that Niko was the European Messiah, let me tell you it was not *all* peaches and honey. The man hid a terrible addiction.

At first, I thought he was going to the bathroom every two seconds, but, in fact, he was the worst chain-smoker I'd ever met. The man couldn't make it through his *own* dinner without having to run outside for a smoke.

"Sweetie . . . I have no time for sex, so leave me my little pleasure," he said when I complained.

I compared the tasks Niko plowed through while squeezing in twenty or so two-puff cigarette breaks to those of the rest of my team and saw that he was still managing double the workload.

"Smoke your brains out," I said.

He did try to quit once. He arrived from brunch with

needles in his ears from acupuncture, having just left a hypnotist, with a Smokers Anonymous meeting set for later in the day. Sadly, the stress of all those appointments caused him to light up.

On something of a whim, I asked Niko-la to go to New Orleans with me. The few days we spent there were easy, fun, deep, and light all at the same time, although sitting next to him as he reveled in the pleasure of being able to smoke at the dinner table was not something I cared to do again.

I did learn that the dark shadows under his eyes were caused by something far more troubling than lack of sleep. The haunted city of New Orleans suited his own dark past.

It's not for me to share any of that, so I'll just say that this guy had more reasons to complain than just about anyone I've ever met. As a champion kvetcher, it's hard for me to admit that anyone has more right to complain than I do, but even I must bow down to a greater victim of life's tragedies now and then.

Mornings in our kitchen were often a bitchfest, with Shimi, the king of hot air, at the top of the heap. He was in his midforties and still upset about things he hadn't gotten when he was two. There's just got to be a statute of limitations on this stuff.

While the rest of us wallowed in undeserved self-pity, producing nothing but a big cloud of negativity, Niko produced the best sauces of the day.

I would turn around after a monologue about my various stages of nausea, sinus blockages, and constipation to see three steaming sauces already cooling.

"Sweetie," he would say to my shocked face, "I come here to work, not talk about what hurts. What does not? Everything hurts. This is life . . . so forget it. Make some gorgeous food!"

When I moved from Long Island City into a dilapidated pizza joint on the Lower East Side that I renovated into a swank commercial kitchen, tasting room, and art gallery, Niko became my head chef, kitchen manager, therapist, and bodyguard. It didn't take long for him to develop his own catering business as well, and it flourished.

Thankfully, his loyalty kept him at my side, often hiring other chefs to send to his own parties, sometimes, I realized, paying them more than I paid him.

One day, while setting up for a quiet party, there was nothing to do but check messages on our cell phones or flirt with the waiters. I asked Niko to make some butter plates.

His brilliant blue eyes grew wide as he smirked, stroking his goatee. The just-fed-cat grin spread across his face.

"Sweetie," he said, "I believe you know that my butter plate days are over. But don't worry. I have trained the entire staff to make them quite lovely."

I knew it was too good to be true.

# N'awlins Vacation Barbecue Sauce

*Serves up to 12 people, depending on what you put it on*

**INGREDIENTS**
*1 white onion, chopped*
*A few pinches garlic, minced*
*1 shot bourbon*
*1 shot balsamic vinegar*
*2 hefty scoops tomato paste*
*A few drizzles Worcestershire*
*1 generous drizzle Tabasco*
*A couple of spoonfuls molasses*
*Salt and fresh ground pepper*
*1 pinch cayenne pepper*

Sauté onion. When it starts to brown, throw in a few pinches of minced garlic. Let this cook for a spell, and hit it with a shot of bourbon. After the bourbon cooks off, throw in a shot of balsamic vinegar.

Let this cook for a minute, then throw in a couple of hefty scoops of tomato paste, a few drizzles of Worcestershire, a generous drizzle of Tabasco, and enough water to thin the paste to a nice sauce-like consistency.

Stir over a low simmer for about 10 minutes, then add a couple of spoonfuls of molasses to sweeten things up. Season to taste with salt, pepper, and cayenne pepper.

This is great as a baste over steak, chicken, shrimp—almost anything that you want to barbecue—or served as dip with some Cajun fries or chicken fingers.

# Jump-to-It Jambalaya

*Serves 4 to 6 people*

### INGREDIENTS

*1 large white onion (or 2 small), chopped*
*A good few drizzles olive oil*
*1 handful celery, diced*
*1 plop garlic, minced*
*1 bell pepper, diced*
*1 coffee cup canned tomatoes (Use whole tomatoes and crush them by hand in a bowl)*
*1 pinch fresh or dried oregano, thyme, and parsley*
*Salt and fresh ground pepper*
*2 pinches cayenne pepper*
*1 coffee cup uncooked white rice*
*3 coffee cups chicken broth*
*1 heaping handful Andouille sausage, diced*
*About 1 lb. shrimp, peeled and deveined*
*1 heaping handful smoked ham or smoked turkey, cubed*
*2 good smidgens Cajun spice or Creole seasoning*

### OPTIONAL

*Cod, clams, mussels, and calamari*

On medium-high heat, sauté chopped onions in olive oil until soft. Then throw in a handful of celery, a plop of minced garlic, and one diced bell pepper. Sauté a few more minutes, then add a coffee cup of whole crushed tomatoes. Season with a pinch each of oregano, thyme, parsley, pepper, cayenne pepper, and Cajun or Creole seasoning, and simmer for a few minutes.

Stir in one coffee cup of uncooked white rice and 3 coffee cups of chicken broth. Lower heat to medium and cover pot, making sure to stir every so often, for about 25 minutes.

When the rice seems like it's mostly cooked, stir in diced Andouille sausage, peeled and deveined shrimp, and cubed smoked ham (smoked turkey is nice too). Simmer until the shrimp is cooked (about another 10 minutes). You can adjust seasoning with salt at this point, but don't before as the Cajun or Creole seasoning may be salty. Adjust pepper, cayenne pepper, and Cajun or Creole as you like it.

At this point, I like to pour the whole shebang into a baking dish. You can either keep it warm or put it in the fridge and, when you're ready to serve, pull out and bake at 350 till hot. Serve this with a few biscuits if you want. You don't need much else, except cold beer and a trusted friend.

If you're in the mood for a heavy seafood jambalaya, throw in a few handfuls of chopped cod filet, clams, mussels, calamari—whatever kind of fish you love—just 10 minutes before you serve it.

# Sandy, the Sauce, and Feminists

The water had receded, leaving behind a brown film on the tiled floor of our lobby on East Eleventh Street. I opened the door to the basement. The twelve feet of stairs that had been completely submerged in brown gruel eight hours before were now half-exposed. Recycling bins, shoeboxes, bicycles, children's toys, and the many possessions of mine and my neighbors that we'd kept in storage floated in the dank, rotting soup.

Thirty years of memories floated in that soup.

Photographs of buffets I'd created in my early catering days in New York City, clippings of magazine stories I'd written, cookbooks I bought in my early chef days when I didn't know the difference between a vinaigrette and a vignette, the acrylic canvases I'd labored over as a teenager, and somewhere, underneath it all, the vintage copy of *The Catcher in the Rye* that inspired me to pluck on as runaway street-kid renegade. It was all there, somewhere beneath the surface, like fragments of my memory floating just below my consciousness.

My mother's college graduation photo was somewhere

beneath the ruined construction material and mud and salty water and possibly sewage. As if trying to save her again, I started down the stairs. Electric wires floating like eels on the brown water made me stop. I couldn't hold on to my mother. I could barely hold on to the railing.

I turned around and walked out onto the street, but I couldn't shake the image of her young, beautiful face floating in the ruin.

All the cars on Eleventh Street had a surreal, misty fog on their windshields. Some of them were still half-filled with water.

The heavy wooden garbage bins that normally sat firmly in the front of my building had floated to the middle of the street and broken into shards of wet, splintered hunter-green wood. The garbage cans they'd held captive were nowhere to be seen.

It was October 30, 2012, the morning after Hurricane Sandy hit New York City. My home in the East Village had been designated Evacuation Zone A.

We lost power, heat, hot water, phones, Internet, and our sense of humor. I was tempted to hail a cab to anywhere that wasn't underwater and call it a day, but twelve blocks away on Houston Street, my commercial kitchen was waiting for me.

The squatters on Avenue C had set up barbecues outside and were grilling and serving all the food donated to them. I gave them an armload of cheese.

"All right! The blond lady gave us cheese!" the grill man yelled.

The grill man, a large, long-bearded man with a joint

hanging out of his mouth, was shouting merrily to all who passed by, "Hungry? Come on over!" It was a marvel to watch yuppies, college kids, tough guys from the projects, drunks, and moms with their toddlers line up together.

Trudging down Avenue C, I saw restaurant owners and their workers out on the street, trying to pull ruined inventory out of flooded basements. Neighbors clustered around trying to help, sometimes forming human conveyer belts to pass dripping sacks of unrecognizable edibles to the sidewalk. I passed a bar where workers hauled kegs of beer and wooden chairs from their watery grave. Someone's couch was in the middle of the street.

The closer I got to Houston Street, the more my heart sank. What would I be walking into when I got to my beloved kitchen?

I suppose it's madness to say that in the middle of all that ruin, I started to think about mango ginger sauce. But it called to me. I made it by spending a day dicing mangoes and red bell pepper, mixing in minced ginger, passion fruit puree, champagne vinegar, chili flakes, salt, pepper, sugar, and love, then cooking it for a little less than forever. It had to have the perfect balance of sweet, salty, spicy, and sublime.

Its companion, the burgundy beef stock, also called. This was the stock that my sous-chef spent three days reducing, adding just a touch of roasted tomato and red wine and then reducing some more.

I threw my head back and started snorting the brisk air for courage.

At sixteen, with a fury fueling me to my core, I had run

away from home. I drew a lot of strength back then from the Janis Joplin lyric, "Freedom's just another word for nothing left to lose."

Three decades later, I wasn't feeling so light.

I had probably lost thirty years of mementos in our basement. I didn't want to say goodbye to my beautiful stainless steel kitchen, too.

As if matters weren't scary enough, I had a party coming up for the fortieth anniversary of *Ms.* magazine. If the feminists of *Ms.* would be tough enough not to cancel, then I wouldn't either, even if it meant cooking their food by campfire. Suddenly, all those years being dragged around the country in a camper by my parents started to feel like boot camp for Sandy.

When I rounded the corner on Houston Street, I heard myself say a prayer.

"Please, please . . . let it be okay."

My adolescent overdose of Judaism had killed the pleasure of praying in any conventional sort of way, but a little request now and then seemed okay.

The lack of power meant our electric gates wouldn't open. I made my way through my dark kitchen from the sidewalk basement entrance with a flashlight. It was like crawling into a cave.

When my feet touched the concrete floor of the basement I heard the sickening sound of my boots hitting water. I felt a dull pain in my stomach.

"Okay, okay, okay!" I heard myself say out loud, then took a deep breath and inched my way forward. It felt familiar, the feeling of stepping into a dark unknown. I remembered the years of being cold and alone, walking the desolate streets of Crown Heights at night. If I could survive that, what was a little wrath of God to slow me down?

I fumbled for my key, trying to hold the flashlight as I opened the inside door. Shining my light along the tiled floor in front of the freezers, I realized the water was only a few inches deep! It had never occurred to me that my business was on an incline. I wanted to find the source of that hill and kiss it. I let out a loud, *"Thank God!"* Then I remembered the food. Six freezers, one walk-in, one low-boy fridge, and two reach-ins were filled to capacity, and there was no power.

On the battery-operated radio my girlfriend Lydia and I had been listening to, they'd said keeping the freezer doors shut would keep food preserved for forty-eight hours, but the Con Edison worker on the street said it would be at least four days before we had power.

I started hauling things out to the sidewalk. A young Puerto Rican woman with three children walked by. I gave her twenty pounds of chopped beef.

I gave away beef roasts, buckets of crabmeat, and whole pastramis. For a few hours, I was a Jewish Santa Claus.

"Take it! Take it! Feed your family!" I screamed to anyone who wanted to eat.

I coerced my landlord (by way of three filet mignons and four sides of salmon) into bringing in a generator, and I hired Stan the Serbian Super to patrol. A generator filled with gas was preferable to a bag of crack during that week. We only had enough power to save one freezer, and I was obsessed with saving the sauces.

Later on, Lydia and I braved the traffic-lightless thirty-block walk uptown where we could get cell phone and Internet reception. *Ms.* magazine had not canceled!

I lined up two emergency kitchens—one in Long Island City for food prep and one in the kitchen of the church where the event would be held. "Get ready to move Mount Olympus!" I announced to Lavelle, my kitchen manager, who could carry a refrigerator on his back as easily as a knapsack and had the kindest soul I have ever encountered.

A few days later, just as we were about to relocate, Con Edison turned the power on. The cheers coming from around my hood felt like a thousand New Year's Eves. It was electrifying! We wouldn't have to relocate, and the sauces would be saved.

My chefs and I were so busy congratulating ourselves that we neglected to notice a nor'easter had blown in, but the stoic women of *Ms.*, pioneers of women's rights, still didn't cancel.

We salted the sidewalk, seared the tuna, grilled the Korean Barbecued Beef, and blazed on through.

The party was a smash. Snow covered and red faced, they came in droves. The Landmark Church on the Upper West Side quickly filled with hungry feminists. It was thrilling to watch the crowd devour my hors d'oeuvres. The portobello sliders were a particular hit.

Everyone seemed relieved to have something to celebrate. It felt like this party was the finish line for surviving the hurricane. From the first terrifying moment of watching my neighborhood go underwater, I had postponed freaking out. But in the middle of the *Ms.* party, looking out at all the happy women dipping grilled shrimp into the mango ginger sauce I'd fought so hard to save, I started to feel my knees go weak. I remembered that one of the great matriarchs of *Ms.*, Pat Carbine, had invited me to speak to the crowd.

The speech I'd prepared was on my computer, which after losing power, the Internet, and my mind, was also lost.

I found my way to the podium and began to stammer along with what I recalled of my speech.

But then I thought about all I had witnessed in those last days of hurricane hell and just went with it.

I talked about the tough women on my block who were feeding the community, heroism in the form of a hot cup of coffee brewed over a gas stove. I talked about Maristela, the Italian mama with the ruined restaurant on my block. Bundled up and stamping her feet to stay warm, she stood guard as night crept over the lightless block.

I thought of my mother and how her years of schnorring (kind of like a cross between bargaining and being cheap) had somehow instilled in me a fierce pride.

"You can do anything Shana Madelah!" she used to say.

I talked about how knowing I was about to help the great ladies of feminism celebrate their anniversary had given me the strength to get through the storm of the century. The applause felt like two hundred hugs.

Gloria Steinem, whom I was now feeding for the second time in my career, came up to me afterward and said, "I loved your speech! Wonderful!"

This was the golden trophy at the finish line, I thought as I hugged her.

I stumbled back into the kitchen, dazzled.

Amy, one of my favorite waiters, stuck her head behind the kitchen curtain and yelled, "Rossi! Wow! You really are a feminist!"

I looked at her, smiled wearily, and said, "Feminist? Shmeminist! Did they like the mango ginger sauce?"

"Yes . . . yes! They loved it!"

"Praise the lord!" I cried, and started plating the French macaroons.

## Mango Ginger Sauce for
## Not Quite the End of the World

*Serves 20 to 50 people as an hors d'oeuvre dip; freeze
what you don't use*

**INGREDIENTS**

*4 mangoes, peeled and diced*
*1 red bell pepper, diced*
*1 plop ginger, minced*
*2 shots champagne or rice wine vinegar*
*A few pinches chili flakes*
*½ coffee cup passion fruit juice*
*1 heaping handful sugar*
*Salt to taste*

I've never had a fast and hard recipe for our mango
ginger sauce, but it pretty much goes like this:

Start with 4 peeled and diced mangoes. Add one diced
red bell pepper, one plop of minced ginger, 2 shots of
champagne or rice wine vinegar, a few shakes of chili
flakes, and ½ a coffee cup of passion fruit juice. Cook
the whole shebang over medium to low heat until the
mangoes are super soft. Give it at least an hour or
longer, dears. Then puree the sauce, but not too much—
you want to keep it chunky and adjust with a lot, I mean
a lot, of sugar. Then add salt just to even things out.

I play with the sugar until I don't feel the bite of the
vinegar anymore and then add salt just to bring it to

the savory side of sweet. Every chef I have worked with makes this differently. It's a give-it-your-own-spin kind of thing. I go heavier on the vinegar and salt. My chef Eran likes to skip the vinegar altogether and play with the chili flakes, salt, and sugar for a holy trio of awesomeness. I had another chef who always threw in mint, and that was also great. Many times, we make it without passion fruit juice, and that's also still pretty darn good. Make it your own!

# The Last Road Trip

The last road trip I took with my parents was in 1989.

To this day, I can't recall how it was that my parents coerced me into joining them on this vacation, but I assume they used the method that had proved enormously effective throughout my childhood: guilt.

I was twenty-five. It had been nine years since I moved out on my own and ten since I'd been on a vacation with my parents.

I knew I wasn't anything near the rock 'n' roll teenager I had been last time we traveled together. I wondered if they were anything like the bickering, bargain-hunting, overeating couple I'd known. Let's just say I didn't have to wonder long.

The plan was to spend a week in San Diego, then drive the scenic Pacific Coast Highway to LA, where we would spend another week visiting my brother.

My parents picked me up at the San Diego airport.

"Slovaaaaaah!"

My mother's Yiddish bellow was far louder than the

women making the departure announcements on the intercom.

"Slovah Davida Shana!"

"Hi . . . Mom!" I said, mortified, praying there was no one I knew on the flight.

My mother sat in the wheelchair she'd used since her stroke two years before. She weaved and bobbed and jumped up and down until I couldn't help but think of Ray Charles at the piano.

My father, as always, stood stoically behind her, chewing on something.

I walked to her chair and leaned down to kiss her. She, as always, immediately grabbed the back of my neck and pulled my face down into her ample bosom until I nearly suffocated.

"How was your flight? You didn't eat any treif, did you?"

"Mom, you know I don't keep kosher."

"Shhhh. I'm pretending I didn't hear that."

"Are you hungry?" asked my father, still gnawing on the mysterious food item he'd been chewing since 1972.

"Yes, actually, I am. How 'bout we drive to the beach and eat somewhere on the ocean?"

My mother frowned, opened up her pocketbook, and dug through a pile of papers.

"I don't have any coupons for that!" she screamed.

"Mom," I groaned.

"I have coupons for Wendy's," she said.

"Mom. I didn't fly all the way to California to eat at

Wendy's. I want to eat somewhere I can't eat at in New York."

She reached into her bag again and finally, after much rustling, looked up with a wide grin on her face.

"We'll go to Sizzler. I have coupons, and I think they even offer a senior citizen discount."

"Mom. They have Sizzlers up north."

"Not like here. They give a California twist to their salad bar. It's completely different."

I sighed, knowing I had lost the battle. Instantly, I remembered what every gastronomic experience had been like growing up in my family.

The year they included Hardee World coupons in the tourist magazines was the worst. All five members of my family—Mom, Dad, Matt, Lil, and I—were sent into every Hardee World we came upon with a dollar-off coupon and twenty-five cents.

Our mission was to order up to $1.25 worth of food and only have to pay a quarter. If we managed to get our meal for $1.05, we could keep the twenty cents.

No matter how hungry we were that vacation, if there wasn't a Hardee World in sight, we had to hold out till we found one. Likewise, no matter how stuffed we were, my mother demanded we eat more if a bright orange Hardee World sign awaited two exits away.

Hardee World gave the McDonald's menu a Southern spin, serving mini pecan pies instead of apple turnovers. After that vacation, ten years passed before I could be in the same room with a pecan, and to this day, the color orange gives me gas.

*My parents (around 1950).*

I had been living in New York City. I was tough, I was gritty, and there was no way a five-foot-tall, 250-pound sixty-two-year-old in a wheelchair was going to tell me what to eat!

"Go back for more; it's all you can eat," she demanded at Sizzler.

"Yes, Mom," I said, shoulders slumped down around my hips.

My family had by this point been trying aggressively to get me to leave New York City and move to California. My brother had moved to LA three years before, and most of my father's family lived in Southern California.

The day my parents purchased a house in a suburb of San Diego and put their New Jersey house on the market, I knew the pressure would be on.

They offered to set me up in my own business if I would relocate to California. At first, it sounded tempting: fully finance me in a business venture? Upon further scrutiny, that business was a kosher deli.

"The world can always use a good kosher deli," my mom had said.

"I'm a chef, Mom!"

"What do chefs make? They make food. What do kosher delis serve? They serve food."

I gave up, remembering a similar fight I'd had with my mother during which she had insisted there was no difference between a writer and a secretary.

"They both type!" she'd insisted.

After being force-fed enough macaroni salad, California-style, which meant, I suppose, that it had beans in it, it was time to go to our motel.

"Did you book something on the beach?" I asked, trying to feel hopeful.

"Close enough," my father said, still chewing.

"Do they have a pool?" I asked, feeling the macaroni churning in my stomach.

"I don't know," my mother said, utterly perplexed at the question. "But they have free breakfast!"

The motel, as it turned out, was on a highway somewhere outside of San Diego proper. The only things it seemed to be near were a discount clothing store and a gas station. The beach was a thirty-minute drive. So was, it would appear, anything one might call attractive.

The place was called the Golden Coach or something like that. It was hard to tell because so many of the letters in the sign were missing. I remember it as the Golden Roach, which it may well have been, for reasons that later became clear.

It did have a pool, but it hadn't been used in about a decade. A swamp-like substance that glowed green filled the cracked orifice that once was a pool. Two young Mexican women lay on lounge chairs near the slime, smoking cigarettes and drinking beer through straws.

At least I was not forced to share a room with my parents. But my adjacent room had far too little in the way of soundproofing, so not only did I have to hear my parents fight about whether or not Wendy's gave a senior citizen discount but I also had to hear a couple having loud sex on the other side. The loud-sex couple was far easier to take.

Although the motel was miles from the nearest anything, my parents were impressed with the fifty-a-night rate, and the free breakfast was the discounted icing on the cheap cake.

"They even have twenty-four hours of free coffee in the lobby," my father said, chewing.

Breakfast was served in the lobby, a rust-colored room that smelled of bug spray. The breakfast buffet consisted of still-frozen Lender's bagels, jars of jam, and frozen butter pats. I almost dislocated a shoulder attempting to tear open a semifrozen bagel to stick it in the toaster.

There was the promised bitter coffee in Styrofoam cups and orange juice that tasted like the can from which it had come.

I covered my bagel with jam to kill the taste of freezer burn and sat in the corner so I could get a good view as the Mexican girls poured rum into their coffees.

My parents had already eaten, having awakened two hours early to make sure to get anything that might potentially run out. When I knocked on the door to their room after breakfast, I saw a dozen Lender's bagels and pats of butter on the dresser.

"For later," my mother said, smiling.

Big S lived in San Diego, where she now cooked for rock concerts. Her earth-mama quality appealed to the bands for whom she cranked out Southern-style comfort food.

"The harder the rocker, the more they love my mac and cheese!" she said, last time we spoke.

After enduring two days of fast food and something that crawled into my pillowcase at night and bit my cheek, I told my parents I was going to spend a couple of days with Big S.

"I'll meet you back here well in time for the trip to LA," I said.

Big S pulled into the roach motel, driving her car, the Thing, and honking like she was in a wedding procession. "Honey, you are about to have yourself some fun!"

My dad sat in the front seat of our car, leaving my mom to watch me from her wheelchair in the center of the parking lot. I grabbed my bag and threw it into the back of Big S's Thing. All of a sudden, Mom wheeled herself toward me so quickly, she nearly sent me flying into the backseat.

"Mom, what is it?"

"Slovah," she said, barely above a whisper.

"Yeah, Mom."

"Have . . . fun . . . "

"I will, Mom. . .You, too. Try to do something different."

I climbed into the jeep and rolled down my window to wave, the guilt seeping into my skin like arsenic.

My mom still sat in the parking lot, staring. I'd forgotten the slate-gray hue her eyes took on in sunlight.

She stood up from the chair and walked to the car window. Mom could walk a little bit, but she preferred the attention the chair got her, especially in airports and shopping lines.

She bent down, using the car window to steady herself and whispered, "Take me with you."

I started to laugh. Mom had always been such a joker, after all, but as Big S started the engine and pushed the stick shift into first, I took another look at my mother standing in the parking lot, watching us pull away. I wasn't so sure it was a joke this time; she'd been watching me drive away for nine years.

"Your mom is a pisser!" Big S said.

"Yeah," I said, trying to remember if I'd ever seen that look in my mother's eyes before. It tugged at me, old and familiar, like a question I'd been asked a lifetime ago and had never answered.

Big S took me across the border into Mexico, where we ate twenty-five-cent fish tacos and drank margaritas. "Straight up, darling; you don't want the ice in this town!"

She took me to Ensenada, where the only tourists rode motorcycles or chewed tobacco. For theater, we visited Ensenada's version of a strip club and watched Mexican women dressed in seventies one-piece bathing suits do something that looked like a cross between runway and the cha-cha.

We spent the night in a hotel on the bay. From my window, I saw dolphins jumping.

When I met up with my parents a few days later, my mother seemed more like her old self, taking charge of packing up the hotel room, ordering my dad around. She greeted me with a fast kiss and slap on the tush.

"Let's hit the road!" she said, laughing.

The drive to LA was beautiful, even if we could only stop at Burger Kings for free burgers with lettuce, tomato, and mayo, hold the burger, which was my mom's way of using her free burger coupons for lettuce and tomato sandwiches.

But I came to understand as we drove along and my mother chatted maniacally about an assortment of dead relatives that I'd missed something, a fleeting chance, a window.

*"Take me with you."*

I've often wondered just what would have happened if I had.

# Mama Harriet's Hungarian Goulash

*Serves 4 to 6 people*

### INGREDIENTS

*2 lbs. cubed stew meat*
*1 drizzle olive oil or vegetable oil*
*A few good pinches salt, fresh ground pepper, dried*
   *oregano, and paprika*
*2 heaping handfuls white onion, sliced or diced*
*1 (8 oz.) can tomato sauce, any variety*
*Water enough to keep things wet—2 coffee cups should*
   *do it*
*1 plop garlic, minced*
*1 good pinch celery salt*
*2 handfuls peeled carrots, sliced or diced*
*1 (16 oz.) package egg noodles (Mom's way) or 2 coffee*
   *cups of cut-up potatoes, any kind*

Start out with 2 lbs. of cheap cubed meat 'cause anything pricey is just a shame, darlings.

Get a heavy-bottom pot hot and drizzle in a little olive or vegetable oil. Season the meat well with salt, pepper, oregano, and paprika, then brown it in the pot. I like to sauté my onions in a separate pot and throw them in with the browning meat, but I'm pretty sure you could just cook them together if you only have one pot or feel lazy. You'll want 2 heaping handfuls of sautéed onions.

When your meat and onions look nice and brown, almost burned, pour in a can of tomato sauce, a coffee cup of water, a plop of minced garlic, a good pinch of celery salt, and 2 handfuls of carrots. Reduce to a simmer and cover. Now cook for an eternity, a good 2 hours, 2½ is even better. You'll probably need to add water and stir every half hour.

If you want potatoes, throw them in for the last half hour of cooking, or do as Mama Harriet did and spoon the meat and vegetables over boiled, Jewish-style egg noodles.

# The "Two Drops and a Plop" Impatient Cook's Glossary

I hate complicated recipes, dishes that require that soul-crushing thing called a measuring cup. All of my recipes are cooked with a shake, a shimmy, and a lot of tasting. They are meant to be improvised, individualized, and played with.

**Smidgen:** What fits between your thumb and forefinger without falling out.

**Pinch:** Pretty much the same thing as a smidgen, but sometimes I just like to say "pinch."

**Handful:** Self-explanatory. But we're talking about a normal, adult-size hand, not your toddler's hand and not Godzilla's hand.

**Plop:** A little more than a tablespoon.

**Drizzle:** Sort of like two wet plops.

**Dollop:** A heaping tablespoon or a plop and a half.

**Sprinkle:** A smidgen, plus whatever falls out.

**Shot:** What lands in your shot glass if the bartender likes you.

**Coffee cup:** Sort of like a cup, only a leeeeetttllleee bit more. Bonus: you can drink "coffee" out of it while your supper simmers.

# Acknowledgments

I must give a special thank you to Lydia DeLisi for filling a void in my heart that I didn't know was there until one day I awoke to find butterflies dancing where cobwebs had been. One thousand thank yous to Nancy Murrell, my literary superhero for sixteen years. Thank God for you. And I have been blessed with one of the kindest editors who walks the earth, Jeanann Pannasch. You believed in me and helped make this dream come true. Thank you.

Gratitude to my dream team: Julia Berner-Tobin, Jennifer Baumgardner, Kait Heacock, and Drew Stevens of the Feminist Press—who I am fairly sure rule the planet.

Thanks also to my beloved mentor, Molly O'Neill, the best foodie mama a cooking and writing girl could have, and a special thank you to Anne Edelstein for her advice and guidance.

A shout-out to my sister, Yaya: now they know, our crazy childhood really did happen!

Thank you to my radio family at WOMR and WFMR in Provincetown for giving me a safe, loving place to tell my stories for nearly twelve years. A piece of my heart to Debbie Stoller and my family at *BUST* magazine for letting me be a part of your dream of helping a woman's spirit fly as high as it wants.

And I must thank the great and magical Arianna Huffington for the *Huffington Post*. It's given me a wonderful world to blog from.

This book is also dedicated to all the brave and crazy women who cooked professionally in the eighties. Rock on, sisters! We made it! It's also for a new generation of powerful young women who can change the world if they want to: Zora Olea Moynihan, Hannah Seitz, Ruby Ross, Tovah Ross, Safia Karasick Southey, and Charlotte Raymond. Go, girls!

And much love to my nephew, Andrew Raymond, for being the closest thing to a son I ever had. You are strong, Andrew. Never forget it.

I have been blessed with so many special friends over the years that have been my family, supporting, guiding, nurturing, loving, and championing me when the world did not. Thanks to my honorary sister Trey Moynihan, my peers Adam Barnett and Alex Alexander (may they rest in peace), Wolf, Broadway bombshell Anne-Marie Gerard Galler, Kristy Parsons, Adeena Karasick, Jenny Weber Zeller, Laura Dubrule, Charmaine Broad, Shelly Spevakow, Lorraine Massey, Charlotte Robinson, Marilyn Rosen, Gus Murphy aka M. Moynihan (RIP), Suzanne Leon, Tom Taylor, Sue Walls, and Chef Eran Dermer. Thank you to the beautiful Melanie Ramsey for teaching me to believe in miracles.

Lastly, for my father Marty, who never got more than

two words in while Mom was alive. Thank you, Dad, for showing me the meaning of an honest day's work. Who knew kosher Chinese egg rolls were the admission ticket to your soul?

I know I forgot someone, so for all my wonderful friends whom I did not mention here, forgive me. Come over and eat!

**The Feminist Press** is a nonprofit educational organization founded to amplify feminist voices. FP publishes classic and new writing from around the world, creates cutting-edge programs, and elevates silenced and marginalized voices in order to support personal transformation and social justice for all people.

See our complete list of books at
**feministpress.org**

**THE FEMINIST PRESS**
AT THE CITY UNIVERSITY OF NEW YORK
FEMINISTPRESS.ORG

As the owner and executive chef of The Raging Skillet, **ROSSI** has earned a reputation as a cutting-edge caterer known for breaking all the rules. The Raging Skillet has been described as "the wildest thing this side of the Mason-Dixon line" by Zagat, a "rebel anti-caterer" by the *New York Times*, and has been named one of *The Knot*'s best wedding caterers six years in a row. Rossi has written for many publications, including *BUST*, the *Daily News*, the *New York Post*, the *Huffington Post*, *Time Out New York*, and *McSweeney*'s. She is the host of the long-running radio show *Bite This* on WOMR and WFMR in Cape Cod and has been featured on the Food Network and NPR.

**31901056559190**